Lois Burpee's Gardener's Companion and Cookbook

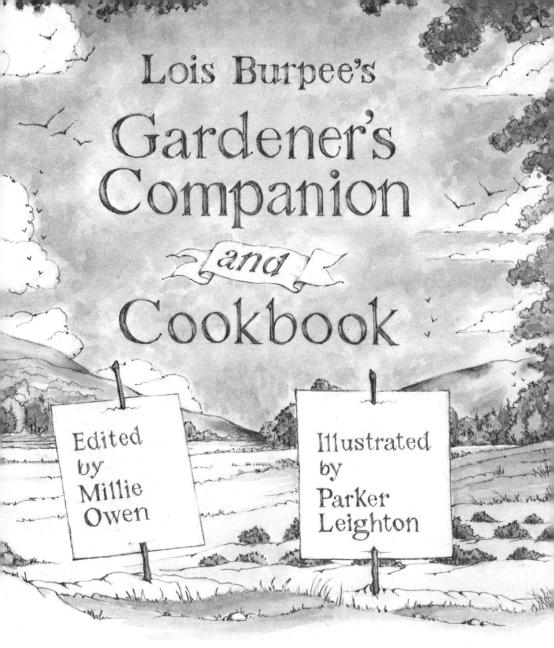

Lois Burpee's Gardener's Companion and Cookbook

Edited by Millie Owen

Illustrated by Parker Leighton

1817

HARPER & ROW, PUBLISHERS

New York, Cambridge, Philadelphia, San Francisco,
London, Mexico City, São Paulo, Sydney

Grateful acknowledgment is made for permission to reprint "Beets with Orange Sauce" from *The World of Vegetable Cookery* by Alex D. Hawkes. Copyright © 1968 by Alex D. Hawkes. Reprinted by permission of Simon & Schuster, a Division of Gulf & Western Corporation.

FIRST EDITION

Drawings by Parker Leighton

Library of Congress Cataloging in Publication Data

Burpee, Lois.
  Lois Burpee's Gardener's Companion and Cookbook
  Includes index.
  1. Cookery (Vegetables) 2. Vegetable gardening.
I. Owen, Millie. II. Title.
TX801.B867   1983   641.6′5   82-47736
ISBN 0-06-038021-7

---

83 84 85 86 87 10 9 8 7 6 5 4 3 2

Contents

Lois Burpee's
Gardener's
Companion
and
Cookbook

1

How I became interested in vegetables.

PARKER LEIGHTON

"How did you, the wife of David Burpee, become interested in vegetables?" is a question frequently asked me—as though I had become a traitor to my husband and his passion for flowers. I am expected to be a flower expert, especially of marigolds, not vegetables. "I just did" is hardly a satisfactory answer. So I got to wondering myself and concluded that perhaps the varied experiences I had with food as I grew from a child—with a child's typical aversion to vegetables—to a homemaker on Fordhook Farms may have had something to do with it.

I was born in Tiberias, Palestine, where my father, a Scot, had founded a medical mission. But I woke up mentally in Glasgow, Scotland, in 1914, when we had to flee from Palestine at the start of World War I. The war limited variety in our food. Meats, sugar, and fats were strictly rationed. (I remember being shocked at a family dinner when an aunt was so bold as to sprinkle sugar on chocolate pudding. We all would have preferred it sweeter, too, but to be so extravagant was unthinkable.) It was a treat when my father, then medical director of the Oakbank Army Hospital, brought home some beef drippings, which we spread on bread as a flavorful substitute for oleomargarine.

The only vegetables I remember being served at dinner besides potatoes were carrots and turnips, and I thought that to like them one would have to have red hair. In a dish in the center of the dining-room table, tangy garden cress grew on wet absorbent cotton. It looked like a tiny forest, and the peppery leaves had a delightful taste. I have recreated this dish of cress many times. It's ready to eat ten days after the seed is planted.

Early in 1919, we came to America to visit my mother's parents in Hartford, Connecticut. Grandma made a delicious crispy pickle of Jerusalem artichokes, which grew in a corner of the backyard. We spent a fairytale summer right next to a real farm in the small town of Winchester. There was so much for me, my three sisters, and my little brother to explore there! Grandpa taught us what berries we could pick, and we walked miles to the best wild strawberry patches. The berries were pretty well mashed by our return, but were still good for shortcake made with hot baking-powder biscuits. We were introduced to corn on the cob, of course, and just couldn't believe that we were really allowed to pick it up in our fingers.

In the fall of 1919, we returned to Palestine on a small steamer. My most vivid recollections of the trip are the flavor of café au lait—made with condensed milk, of course—and a storm in which the bathtub broke loose. The roll of the ship had got the best of me—I was lying on my berth, eyes glued to the porthole, through which I would sometimes see only sky, then the top of the waves, and, for an interminable length of time, only water. At last, with relief, I saw the skyline and sky again, but for far too short a time. A woman's voice shrieking, "The bathtub's broken loose, the bathtub's broken loose," broke the spell that porthole held over me. Fear turned to laughter. We were told later that some of the ship's cargo had also broken loose and slid off center so the ship could not completely right itself. When we finally reached port, it still listed to one side.

Arriving in Tiberias was a broad leap into an entirely new world—not only a new home, but new languages and new foods. I loved the fruits, but, oh my, the strong flavors of the food! Stuffed eggplant was cooked with tomatoes and both ripe and green olives, some of which were quite bitter. Everything seemed to be sour except lentils and bulgur. But the desserts, served only at feasts, were devastatingly sweet. The memory of little hollow doughnutlike balls full of syrup flavored with rosewater still haunts me. They were made from small balls of raised dough, cooked first in hot fat and then in the syrup. I've tried to make them but haven't been able to get the syrup inside. Eating a whole cherry tomato reminds me of them—not the flavor, of course, but what happens in the mouth.

All vegetables that could be eaten raw—radishes, lettuce, carrots, and, of course, tomatoes—were grown in the hospital compound, where they would not become contaminated. The cress that used to grow in the dish on the table in Scotland sprouted in the garden overnight and was eaten in a few days. Then we replanted more cress.

I was miserable for a long time. Breakfast was the only meal I really liked. Of course, I had to eat what I was served. None of this business of "What would you like?" in those days. Gradually, some dishes became not too distasteful. Curiosity got the best of me. Why did people like these strong-flavored foods? Perhaps I would like them, too. I would find out only by tasting.

We children had a large breakfast with fruits and cooked cereal. Lunch, with the adults, was composed of Arabic dishes: stuffed vegetable marrow, which is like zucchini, cooked in leban (a form of yogurt); eggplant and tomato stew; boiled lentils or bulgur with ground lamb or goat; and occasionally stewed rabbit or chicken, which the family raised. We children had our early supper of eggs, bread, and olives. I learned to love olives and also lebanee, which is like cream cheese but more sour. It was kept in olive oil and spread on fresh Arabic bread, then sprinkled with zatre, a dried mixture of sorrel and winter savory.

I was fascinated by what went on in the outbuildings behind the hospital. In one, the washerwomen did the laundry in huge built-in caldrons. They often brought in plants to nibble on, whatever was growing on the hillsides. So I began to look around the compound grounds and take them all sorts of plants to see if they would eat them, too. Often they ate only the succulent inner part of the stem. Some plants, like a daisy-type one, they said were too soapy.

Two other buildings were the hospital kitchens: one for preparing food for the Moslem and Christian patients and staff, the other a spotless kitchen with lots of shiny pots on the walls where meals were prepared for the Jewish patients. My excursions to these were only in the late afternoon on Saturday, because our days were quite regulated. I watched, fascinated, and sometimes tasted the tidbits offered me. Gradually I sort of got to like Arabic food. Years later I had a yen for the flavors I remembered.

Another Saturday pastime for us children was cooking. We had one of the little buildings along the compound wall for a playroom. Among the few toys brought with us from the United States were little cast-iron stoves. We each had one and used charcoal for fuel. We were permitted to use anything that grew in the garden as well as eggs from our chickens. We tested the things the washerwomen ate and roasted all sorts of seeds to see if we could make imitation coffee. I remember clearly one day when I got some salt and added it to the potato and egg mess I was cooking. I proudly announced that salt made it taste better. My older sister squelched my pride by responding, "Melani [the cook] always uses salt!"

After my father's death we came to America again in 1924. By this time Grandpa had retired to the old family homestead in northwestern Connecticut. His occupation now was tending his vegetable garden and one row of sweet peas, which we children had to pick faithfully every other day to keep them blooming. His garden soil was sandy and the season short, but what wonderful vegetables he could grow! And, to my surprise, they were good to eat. Our meals were such traditional New England dishes as fresh peas with young carrots lightly seasoned with a slice of salt pork fat (not smoked) and desserts sweetened with dark molasses. I can still visualize Grandpa poring over the Burpee seed catalog in the winter, planning his next year's garden.

When Mother took over the kitchen, she had to relearn how to cook. There was one huge white cookbook to which she often referred, and the food order was phoned in to the one butcher and one grocer in the town once a week. To save time (or maybe it was an old custom), one large piece of meat was ordered. We had it hot on Sunday, cold on Monday, and what we children called third-day roast on Tuesday. I have followed this tradition in some ways, but have the hot roast on Saturday and the cold meat on Sunday, as I find a day of rest from cooking quite relaxing. The old New England custom of having hot baked beans and brown bread on Saturday and eating them cold on Sunday is really not a bad idea. Instead of cold baked beans, I do something with all the leftover vegetables in the refrigerator, such as making a casserole with a cheese cream sauce.

Grandma made the gingerbread. This was important because Grandpa had to have gingerbread every night for supper. She baked it in a large blackened pan about three inches deep that was almost as large as the oven.

My two older sisters took over the few times when Mother was not home. They objected to my being in the kitchen because they said I was always washing my hands and getting in the way. My oldest sister usually made a cake. One day they were also away. I was to be in charge of preparing dinner (a cold meat day, of course). This was my opportunity to show my cooking prowess. I decided to make a sponge cake, which would not need frosting. I had Grandma's gingerbread pan in mind for baking it in.

So I got out the one big cookbook and looked up the recipe. It called for one cup of flour. How could that possibly make enough for eight people and have some left over? I decided to triple the recipe and increase the amount of lemon extract, as it seemed much too little. I put my batter in the gingerbread pan and placed it in the bottom of the hot oven to bake (I didn't know how to raise the shelf). Soon there was a delightful aroma—then one of burning. I peeked in the oven. The cake was flowing over the edges of the pan. Oh, well I thought, let it bake anyway. I *did* know that I should not disturb a baking cake. The burning smell got stronger and stronger, but it was not yet time to take the cake from the oven.

When the time did come, the cake looked fine on top, but the oven was a mess. All the family returned for dinner, and I proudly served the cake in the large pan. My oldest sister facetiously remarked, "Are we *still* eating this cake?" Of course, it was burnt on the bottom, and the lemon flavor was overwhelming. I was so disappointed. To this day, I can't stand synthetic lemon seasoning, and I seldom bake a cake.

Eight years of boarding school and college menus, and four years of stretching the dollar-a-day budget, while sharing an apartment with a sister or friend in the depression years, were a culinary vacuum, with one exception. While at Wellesley College, I was introduced to Chinese food. A group of students who had lived abroad and had some association with China met for inexpensive dinners in Cambridge or Boston at a Chinese restaurant. Then a friend of one of my college friends opened a Chinese restaurant in Wellesley, and my friend and I visited its kitchen frequently. I was fascinated with Chinese cooking methods and utensils. Everything could be prepared so quickly. These experiences intensified my delight later when I actually had my own vegetable garden.

I was a botany major at college. After graduating in 1934, I spent two years in Baltimore studying. Fortunately, my small apartment was near a farmers' market. I was hoping to find a job in the field of horticulture, and one day I received a letter suggesting that I write to the W. Atlee Burpee Company. As luck would have it, the International Flower show was to be held in Baltimore in a few weeks. The Burpee company would have a booth there and would need temporary help for the duration of the show. It was there that I met David Burpee.

After the show, I was asked to come to Philadelphia for a interview and was given the position of technical correspondent for the Flower Department.

I knew little about flower varieties, so spent many Saturday mornings in the summer studying the flowers in the trials field at Fordhook Farms on the edge of Doylestown, Pennsylvania. Seeds of all the flowers listed in the catalog were test grown along with test rows of the breeding work done in California. There were vegetable trials also, but they were in a distant field. Occasionally Mr. Burpee joined me there.

After a year I was asked to also do library research for Mr. Burpee on the history and development of marigolds and other major classes of flowers, such as zinnias and petunias. To make it easier to have access to the library at the Museum of Natural History, I was given an office and typist in downtown Philadelphia. Occasionally Mr. Burpee stopped in and took me out to lunch. One day, quite unexpectedly, he proposed. For the first time I became aware of his ploy to get me away from everyone at the main office. Soon after, he left for an inspection trip to California and the downtown office was closed.

I came to Fordhook Farm as Mrs. David Burpee in July 1938. Now I had lots of time to spend in the flower rows and also the vegetable trials, but I also had to plan meals. A huge vegetable garden had been planted for the homestead use. It seemed that every vegetable in the catalog was growing there. The gardener brought in baskets of whatever was ready to use (usually larger or beyond the best stage for delicacy) as he had done while Mr. Burpee was a bachelor. Curiosity got the best of me. There were so many vegetables listed in the catalog and growing in the vegetable-testing trial rows that I had never heard of. And why so many varieties—did they have different tastes and textures? I found out that they did. I was fortunate to have an experienced cook in the kitchen, as all this was quite different from my past housekeeping experiences. The following years I selected the seeds to be planted for homestead use and, of course, included seeds for any of the new varieties we were thinking of introducing through the catalog.

The first few years at Fordhook, while our daughter and son were young, I did not do the physical work in the garden but supervised the planting of the seeds so that we would have variety all through the season. The soil here was different from any I had been used to, fine and heavy—even radishes had to be dug, and the root crops were stubby and tough.

Gradually the old gardener retired and I had to become more involved in the garden because my help did not have experience. I was determined to do something about the soil. We had riding horses, plenty of leaves in the fall, and lawn clippings in the summer—why not take advantage of them? So I selected an area of the garden in which to improve the soil. It was a strip twenty feet wide, and this width gave me eighteen-foot rows that were just right for most succession plantings for my household of five to six persons and even some extra for freezing.

This size garden I could almost handle by myself, and it became a pleasure to work in. I did the planting and picking and supervised the weeding. Yes, weeding needs supervision, for so often it disturbs the roots of the vegetables. When the plants are young, I cut the weeds off at ground level with a knifelike tool called a horse's hoof trimmer. The less the soil is disturbed, the better the plants will grow.

As I plant seeds, I think of the size of the seed, what it is to become, and the struggle it will have to come through the earth. When the directions on a seed packet say the plants should be ten or more inches apart and the seeds are smaller than peas, I sow three or four seeds in each of the ten-inch spaces. When the seeds sprout, the groups of seedlings help each other through the soil and there will not be gaps in the row. Later, I cut out the extra plants. Many new gardeners have said that they hate to thin out young plants, but this must be done. Unless a plant has space in which to develop properly, it will not produce because it cannot get enough food.

Poring over the catalog to make out my seed order, I got curious as to how the breeders were making their taste tests, and I learned that they usually tested the vegetables raw as they examined them in the fields. I discussed this with Mr. Burpee, commenting that, since the final use of vegetables was in the home, they ought to be tested as part of a meal. Well, I gave myself quite a job with this suggestion. Now our meals frequently included more than one kind of bean, pea, or beet. Divided vegetable dishes and small garden labels came in handy for identification. We didn't always prefer the new introductions, but we discussed all their qualities— plant habit, ease of picking, and such. We did not find a bean we preferred in flavor to Tenderpod, though others are better producers.

Early on I discovered the Lutz Green Leaf beet, a late, very sweet variety. But it's an ugly duckling, with a tendency to have light rings that breeders do not like. To me the flavor is the best of all beets, and the foliage stays green when cooked, as it does not have a red stem. The company dropped this beet from the catalog one year—and I yelled. It was not a good seller, they said. Of course not, because the description did not point out its best qualities. So they included it again with a more "tasteful" description, and it's still in the catalog. I've found that Lutz Green Leaf is also the favorite of other kitchen gardeners.

Most of Burpee's new vegetable introductions to American gardners came from the Orient, and some indication of how they were cooked there came with them. So I experimented with how they could be prepared in an American home. I also had some help from the kitchen testing department of the *Farm Journal*, a magazine that had a long history of cooperation with the Burpee company. Missionaries from lands to which the vegetables were indigenous sent in more recipes. This was fine, except when I was asked to prepare samples in quantity for the annual garden writers' luncheons. Then it was a job. The writers asked for the recipes, and that is how I really got into vegetable cooking. I was literally challenged into it.

Involvement in cooking also got me interested in herbs, about which I knew little, but I had distinct memories of flavors from Palestine. So I volunteered to give a program on herbs for a small garden club to which I belong. I gave myself plenty of time to do research, and I don't know when I have had more fun with an assignment. I chose to get well acquainted with a few herbs, and then add a new one to my experience each season.

A few years ago an Indian couple stayed with us and introduced me to the use of ginger root and seeds of cumin, coriander, and cardamom with vegetables, rice puddings, and tea. You will find their influence in some of the recipes in this book.

Mr. Burpee was not a cook, but he had definite ideas on menus and combinations of foods that went well together. We always talked over what we would serve our guests. He loved to have fun at parties. One of his favorite jokes to play on his own dinner guests at his club was to pass out a menu printed with the worst combinations he could think of, such as oysters with fudge sauce. Once a guest said, "Excuse me, Mr. Burpee, but do you mind if I leave?"

Our lunches and dinners began with a salad, and vegetables were more important for the main course than meats. We served only one starchy vegetable and often substituted corn, winter squash, salsify, or candied parsnips for the usual potato or rice. I like to have a harmonious color combination on the plate and only one vegetable with a sauce (or no creamed vegetable at all when fatty meats are served). Mr. Burpee did not like mixed-up dishes (which I love), except casseroles made for lunch with leftovers and noodles or rice. Our desserts were made with fruit—apple pie, fruit cobbler, or puddings with fruit sauces. I have always tried to think about the entire meal when planning what to serve, especially when it comes to the dessert. A dessert laden with cream adds too much fat to a roast-beef dinner with all the trimmings.

Our two children, like most, were not enthusiastic vegetable eaters. They preferred their carrots and peas raw. Our daughter Blanche's favorite cooked vegetables were spinach and lima beans; our son Jonathan's, beets. The evening meals were the one time the family was together so I always tried to have some things each person enjoyed. This could be a chore, but I decided I might as well find some way to make a daily task interesting. I did this by thinking of the planning and preparation of a meal as an accomplishment, just as painting a picture would be. I experimented with textures, colors, and tastes and searched for the flavors I remembered from my youth and from pleasant restaurant experiences.

So this is how I became interested in cooking: through the vegetable garden and the challenges presented to me. Writing this book is yet another challenge.

Vegetables deserve a much more important role on menus than they are usually given. They come in far greater variety than meats, and they add interest and color to a meal. I always consider a menu for a meal as a whole, as a flavor, color, and calorie composition. Some flavors clash, just as colors clash. If I am considered a good cook, it may be just because of the flavors, textures, and colors I combine for a meal. This I could not do without vegetables and fruits.

The garden and the cook.

My mouth waters as I browse through the seed catalog in winter, deciding what I am going to grow in my garden. Each year the seed order seemed to get longer and longer. But I have finally learned to cut down.

I once gave a talk on "How to Order from a Seed Catalog," and my husband asked me what I had told my audience. I replied that I had told them that most catalogs specify the length of row a seed packet will plant and that they should keep in mind the size of the garden when deciding on quantity to order. For a family of three or four, a twenty-foot row of some vegetables is too much to plant all at once, but for others, such as beans and peas, it is just right. I told them six tomato plants, two zucchini plants, and three pepper plants would probably be enough. His comment was "You're not helping me to sell seeds."

Maybe I wasn't helping him to sell quantity, but it is better to have happy cooks who are not overburdened with produce each July and August and who enjoy their garden and their summer.

It's easier to plant long rows of beans than to pick the beans and do something with all the ones you can't use that day. My solution is to plant a row length that will provide enough at one picking for a meal for double the size of my family. Then there will be enough for guests or freezing. And I've learned to make succession plantings of lettuce, peas, beets, carrots, and corn. I also make two plantings of summer squash and cucumbers because the bugs or weather often kills off the first planting.

I do make some plantings larger than others and I plan them so they'll be right for picking during vacation time, when I'll have more time for preserving and freezing. Because weather can make a difference in time until maturity (picking time), I allow a two-week leeway.

Planting the garden with vacation dates in mind is important if you want to be as enthusiastic about the garden at the end of the season as you were at the beginning. Most of us have an instinctive desire to store or make use of the very last bit of produce—and during the winter, a store of home-grown vegetables in the freezer is very satisfying—but it is not fun to be pressured during the growing season.

An easy way to make use of just the few extra peas you might have in late June is to put all the peas in a pot of boiling water. After two minutes, take out those you will not need for the meal. Put them in a colander and cool then under cold water. Continue cooking the remaining peas for your dinner; package the extra peas and freeze them. This can be done with other vegetables as well. Freezing does not have to be a big production.

I like to pick vegetables in the cool of the morning when they are crisp. But don't leave them in the garden basket to wilt. Put them in plastic bags without washing, unless they are muddy, and refrigerate. If you have to wash them, which of course is the case with root crops, dry them, bag them, and keep them in a cool place until time for preparation of the meal. This way they will generally keep for two days. Chard and spinach should be used the day they are picked because any torn or bruised leaves turn brown.

In order to get the most from your vegetable plants, it is important to keep picking from all those that produce flower heads, seed pods, or fruits. It's just the same as with flowers. A plant's objective is to reproduce itself, so when a cucumber, squash, or melon plant has developed mature fruits, it stops producing female flowers, which would become the fruits you want. It is a good idea to look over all these plants at least every other day. If a squash has grown larger than you like, do not hesitate to compost it. You will get another. Cucumbers are notorious for not producing when not picked, as are patty pan squash. It is also better to cut off all broccoli heads that have developed beyond an attractive eating size. The plant will again try to reproduce itself and grow more heads, though smaller ones.

The gardener who has beautiful plants and no fruits has probably been too generous with fertilizer. Vegetables whose green parts are eaten or frequently picked, such as chard and celery, require more food than peas, beans, or tomatoes, which you want to flower.

When tomatoes and vine crops have grown big enough, I start tip pruning in order to get better fruits. I figure a melon plant puts more strength into the melons that have formed when I snip off the growing tips of the runners in mid-August.

The beginning gardener-cook will find that the crop pretty much determines the daily menus. The beautiful broccoli head in the garden won't be beautiful four days later, nor will peas be sweet. Garden produce is seasonal, and I enjoy it as such. What to do with a bumper crop is really the stimulus of creative cooking. There are so many different ways to prepare a vegetable that meals do not have to be monotonous when one crop is bountiful. Using an herb, or a seasoned cream sauce, or a different method of cooking—stir-frying instead of boiling—can give variety even with the same vegetable. That is what I hope this cookbook will stimulate a gardening cook to do.

If you do not have space in which to grow a quantity of vegetables, I would certainly still plant a few if your yard gets at least five hours of sun: one or two plants of sweet peppers, one hot pepper, two tomato plants, three okra (which could be in a background planting). And I would have the following herbs: chives, which live over from year to year, three parsley plants, two basil, three oregano, marjoram, and savory or thyme. I would also make two or three plantings of dill a month apart, so as to have nice green dill over a long period—it is so good for dips. All of these plants can also be grown in large containers.

Should there be room for more than these, by all means plant broccoli—it tastes so much better fresh and continues to produce small heads all through the summer. Loosehead lettuce is also good to have, and you can make repeated sowings.

Being a gardener, I associate vegetables with seasons, so when I began writing this book in midwinter, my thoughts started with the anticipation of the spring and early-summer vegetables, then mid-summer and fall, and the book is organized in this sequence. There are some vegetables that just do not grow well in cool weather, such as lima beans, and some that do not grow well in hot weather, such as spinach, peas, and radishes. This too should be kept in mind as you plan your garden.

Some of the vegetables discussed in this book, such as chard, may be available only in your garden, since they do not ship well, or they are not grown commercially because there is little demand for them, such as salsify and celeriac. Others, like celtuce, Malabar spinach, and tampala, were introduced to American gardeners by the W. Atlee Burpee Seed Company and have not yet become well known. One of the great pleasures of gardening is being able to grow, and share, vegetables not available in the markets.

Fresh garden vegetables have flavor of their own unless it is cooked out of them. Boiling breaks down the cell walls of the vege-table, and some of the food values and flavor are released in the water. Therefore, the longer a vegetable is cooked in water the less flavor it will have. If by chance you have prepared a vegetable too far in advance, don't leave it sitting in water. Drain it, put it in a colander or steamer, and keep it warm over hot water, not in it. Cover with a perforated lid so steam can get out, or do not cover.

I do not like to see any water in the bottom of a vegetable serv-ing dish. It means the draining was not complete. Why does this matter? Because the butter used for seasoning really doesn't stay on wet vegetables.

There are two main classes of vegetables, which I treat differ-ently in cooking: those that grow aboveground and are usually green, such as beans, or yellow, such as squash; and those that are a part of the plant that grows underground, such as carrots.

Aboveground vegetables, except for winter squash, are delicate and tender and therefore need your close attention. My objective in cooking vegetables is to retain flavor, nutrients, and color, and to get the degree of tenderness or firmness I want. To achieve this I find I must be at the stove, or nearby, while aboveground vegeta-bles are cooking so that I can frequently taste them. There seems to be a fad today to serve vegetables almost as firm as when they are raw. But I don't think they have the flavor that a little more cooking will give them. This is especially so with green beans, asparagus, and broccoli.

To start with, I always have a kettle of boiling water on the stove. Put prepared green vegetables in a heavy pot and pour boiling water over them to cover. Place on high heat so the water will return to the boil quickly. And ½ teaspoon salt to 2 cups of vegetables (4 cups of raw spinach or other leafy greens). Don't put the lid on, for green vegetables lose their bright green color when covered. Stir them with a fork from time to time so that the cooking will be even. Taste. When they are at the degree of doneness you like, remove them from the stove, drain completely, and put them back in the pot over low heat to steam for about a minute to get rid of excess water. I like peas and lima beans slightly moist, so I do not give them the extra dry steaming. Asparagus, broccoli, and squash should be cooked each in its own way; see discussions of specific vegetables.

The cells of root vegetables contain less water and more substance, such as fiber and starches or sugars, and therefore they take a longer time to cook than aboveground vegetables. But they can be cooked too long—don't let them get soggy. For the best flavor a root should be cooked whole and then cut into serving pieces. If this takes too long, you can retain flavor by using a heavy pot for cooking cut-up root vegetables and barely covering them with boiling water. Cover the pot to conserve heat. It's impossible to say how long to cook them because it all depends on the age and size of the root. I test for doneness by fork or by taste, then drain them well, season them, and put them back on a low burner for a few minutes.

There are many good vegetable cookbooks from which I have learned a lot. One I found in the Burpee homestead is *How to Cook Vegetables,* by Mrs. S. T. Rorer, published in 1892 by the W. Atlee Burpee Company, Seed Growers. It's a most complete book, unfortunately no longer in print. Mrs. Rorer was principal of the Philadelphia Cooking School. It is interesting to note that the only herb she mentions is parsley.

I was delighted, in 1968, to receive a copy of *A World of Vegetable Cookery* by Alex D. Hawkes, published by Simon and Schuster. It's a most attractive, very complete book on vegetables, their origins, and how to prepare them. Mr. Hawkes knows a lot more about cooking than I do, but it was interesting to learn that I had come to some of the same decisions about vegetables on my own.

I have been stimulated by *Try It Cook Book: Fun with Unusual Cooking* by the Benzinger Sisters of Altadena, California (1970). They make good use of herbs. I had been doing a lot of "trying," and it was fun to find out what they had tried. I hope you too will try something different in your garden each year.

The Market and the Cook

Often when I am marketing and passing by the produce counter a friend who does not have a garden stops me and asks, "How can I tell if these vegetables are fresh or this melon is ripe?" You can tell freshness by the brightness of the color, the number of bruises, and the appearance of the skin. Pea pods should be smooth and firm; green beans should snap. If broken ends are brown they are not really fresh. Spinach should be crisp and eggplant and squash firm. A kernel of corn should squirt juice when pierced by a fingernail. The aroma of a melon and a slight yellow tint are better indicators of ripeness than softness at the tip. There should be no stem on a cantaloupe or Crenshaw melon, but a watermelon should have a brownish stem.

My most useful tools.

All through the ages people have thought of ways to make work easier by making tools for specific jobs. In the Mercer Museum in Doylestown there is a marvelous collection of tools used for the farm, home, merchant, and professional trades in Pennsylvania up to the late 1800s. It is fascinating, and it teaches that a specific tool makes a job easier.

Don't struggle with the wrong tool. This is one of my mottoes. It's better to take the time and spend the money to get the right one, for the task—whether in the garden or in the kitchen—will get done more quickly and with less effort.

Tools in the Garden

I have a small but powerful **motor-driven garden tiller** to do the heavy work in the spring and fall. I do intensive gardening, so I looked for the narrowest machine that was not topheavy. When plants are growing, the earth around their roots should not be disturbed; after the garden is planted, the tiller blades should get no closer than six inches from the plants and should not cultivate deeply.

Half the pleasure of being outdoors is to hear the birds, so I prefer quiet tools, like a **man-powered cultivator.** Also I'm sure I am keeping myself in better physical and mental health by using my own muscles. The proper way to use a cultivator is with a forward-backward movement, not a steady forward push. This is excellent exercise for the upper body. There are several kinds of cultivators on the market, and I have two of them.

A one-wheeled cultivator, sometimes called a "firefly," with a furrow plow can save much time. I use it to make straight furrows before planting seeds and also for covering up larger seeds, such as beans, after planting. When setting out plants 6 inches tall or more, I place the plants on one edge of a furrow and use the plow to push soil over the roots. I use it through the growing season to push soil up over beets, and for all plants when heavy rains have washed soil away from their roots.

My other quiet cultivator, a Ro-Ho Gardener, has a horizontal bar which, when the cultivator is held correctly, cuts small weeds at the soil surface and loosens only the top of the soil. Too much water is lost from the garden when the soil between plants is dug up, but an inch of loose soil conserves moisture. This type of cultivator is also an excellent weeder if used when weeds are still in the seedling stage. This is when it is easiest and best to get after weeds— before their roots have grown and devoured your fertilizer.

Of course, a **hoe** was invented before cultivators and is also needed. There are all kinds of hoes—make sure you have the right one for you. When you hold it on the ground, a garden hoe blade for weeding and cultivating should slant toward you and not be at a right angle to the soil. It is not a chopper but a cutter, so a hoe needs sharpening now and then. If you are a short person, have the handle cut off to suit your comfort.

A **hone** for sharpening the hoe and other garden tool blades is essential.

You may want a wide **rake** and a narrow one. I find the narrow one easier to use around growing plants. Never leave a rake on the ground with the sharp tines up, lest someone step on them.

A **shovel** with a blade 6 by 8½ inches makes just the right-size holes for transplanting tomato, cabbage, and pepper plants, and using a shovel is so much easier on the gardener than making holes with a trowel.

You need more than one **trowel,** for sometimes one gets mislaid no matter how careful you think you are. I like the narrow-bladed ones. Do not buy the cheapest, for their blades separate from the handles in no time. The shank of the blade should be part of the handle. The thicker the handle the easier it is on your hand. To keep my hand from aching, I use a section of foam pipe insulation on the handle, which gives a nice soft grip. Do not lay a trowel down—always stick it up in the soil so you will see it quickly.

A **pronged hand cultivator** is handy when working close to plants and loosening young perennial weeds which persist in a strawberry patch or asparagus bed.

I use a **garden cart** with large wheels. The larger the wheels the easier it is to push or pull. When I go to my garden, which is not right next to the house, I load my cart with all the tools and watering cans.

An **apron** with large pockets—how much time this saves! The pockets hold my seed packets, pencil for marking labels, small clippers, and often something to tie up plants.

Save old **stockings.** They are very good for tying tomatoes or other plants to stakes; they are easy on the plant, strong, and not as conspicuous as strips of cloth. They can be cut lengthwise.

Save a **can with a metal lid** and punch holes in it to use when applying rotenone dust to cabbages, corn silk, and other vegetables that worms like. A **plant duster** is also useful for insect control.

Tools in the Kitchen

As with all kinds of handwork, having the right tools for the job makes work in the kitchen much easier and pleasanter. Here are the items that I find essential or preferable for cooking.

Good sharp knives are a necessity. I use one with a short blade for peeling or cutting ends off beans; a wide ten-inch blade, sometimes called a chopping knife, for cutting carrots or celery; a serrated blade for cutting plants from their roots, such as spinach and lettuce. Use a stainless steel knife when cutting something acid, such as rhubarb. I think it makes a difference in the flavor, and it certainly does on the knife.

I place knives on a magnetic holder so I can always keep track of them. Please do not keep knives in a drawer. It is bad for the knives and your fingers. A rolling knife sharpener does an excellent job of sharpening. I keep one in my utensil drawer.

When you take a knife to the garden it is a good idea to put something bright on its handle, such as nail polish or freezer tape, so it is readily seen should you put it down. Always stick the blade into the soil rather than laying it down.

A **cutting board** with a handle is useful to take cut vegetables to the pot.

A **vegetable peeler,** preferably the sharp swivel-bladed kind that has a frencher at the end, is good for peeling fruit as well as vegetables. I hate to see anyone use a knife to peel potatoes. So much is wasted, including the trace minerals that are close to the skin. Be sure to dry the peeler after each use (they are usually not stainless), especially if you have used it on acid fruit.

After preparing vegetables, I put them in a **colander on feet** for a good washing before cooking. A colander may also be used for draining after cooking, but I prefer to use a **pot strainer,** which is a crescent-shaped strainer on a handle that is held over and against the edge of the pot when pouring off liquid. This is also a great time and heat saver because the vegetables stay right in the hot pot. It drains much more thoroughly than when you hold a lid lightly against the pot, and you can see what you are doing.

A **granny fork**—a three-pronged fork with a wooden handle— is useful for testing doneness. Testing should not be done with a sharp-pointed knife—it can penetrate vegetables when they are still too firm.

A pair of **kitchen scissors** can be used for snipping chives, parsley, celery leaves, other green leaf seasonings, and cooked asparagus.

I use a **slotted lifter** with a very slightly curved or flat bottom edge for stirring anything that needs mixing or might stick to the bottom of a pan, such as cream sauces. I recently acquired a conical wire whisk—flat on the bottom—which also does a good job of mixing. Don't use a spoon—too little of its surface meets the bottom of the pot.

A **double boiler,** preferably stainless steel, enameled, or Pyrex, is useful for preparing sauces and desserts that should not come to a boil.

To keep vegetables warm before serving, use a **rustproof strainer** that will fit into a pot over water, then cover.

A **spatter lid** allows steam to pass through. Use it for covering vegetables that are being held in a strainer until time to serve.

A **two-cup pot** marked with cup measurements is very handy when adding liquids for hot sauces.

A **grater** is the precursor of today's food processors. The four-sided kind is convenient to use but difficult to clean, so I use flat graters with different-size cutting holes and slicers.

The **food processor** is most convenient when preparing foods for a number of people. However, I prefer to use my sharp wide-bladed knife and a cutting board when cooking for two.

A **food mill** is helpful in preparing cooked tomato juice, applesauce, or other strained foods. It is a metal strainer that rests on the rim of a container. Its wide blade is turned in the center, pressing food through disks with holes of various sizes.

Put old **newspapers** on the table when you sit down to peel or prepare a lot of vegetables. Let all the pieces to throw away or compost fall on the paper. When through, all you have to do is roll up the paper, and everything is tidy in a jiffy.

Some other items, though not exactly tools, are useful in the kitchen: A roll of **paper towels** is handy for drying parsley, holding hot potatoes or beets when peeling, and all sorts of other uses. **Plastic scouring pads,** the rough flat kind, are good for cleaning baking potatoes, young carrots, salsify, and Jerusalem artichokes. Use **aluminum foil** for lining a broiling pan, especially when basting meats with anything containing sugar, or when you want to clean up in a hurry.

Seasoning:
in search of a taste.

Cooking is like creating a flavor picture or composition. The dominating flavor should be that of the vegetable or meat, and the seasoning a complementary or surprising touch.

The seasonings I use in cooking are based on acquired or remembered tastes associated with a specific food. The pleasure of that subtle difference a bit of wine adds has been acquired. The flavors of foods of my youth, such as mint in potato salad and brown crisped onions with lentils, are all remembered. Then there is that extra touch that brings out taste, as lemon juice can do, or gives a pleasant surprise, such as toasted pine nuts in rice or bits of green olive in a mixed dish.

A friend said to me, "If you write a cookbook please tell us how much seasoning to use." That's very hard to do with vegetables. Most gardeners don't know the measure of the quantity they are cooking, so vegetable seasoning usually is by size of pot, experience, and tasting. Tasting is most important. I was told as a child that it is an insult to the cook to shake salt over your food before tasting. Extra salt should not be necessary if the cook has tasted the food.

I can't tell when vegetables are sufficiently cooked without tasting, even though I know about how long they usually take. Tomatoes vary so much in acidity and taste it's most important to taste stewed tomatoes. A bit more sugar and a pinch of nutmeg or all-spice might give the exact flavor you relish. A soup might be a bit thin or flat-tasting. Adding a teaspoon of cornstarch dissolved in a little soup liquor just pulls it together, and a cube or teaspoon of broth bouillon counteracts blandness. I sometimes add a light sprinkling of mixed salad herbs.

When adding seasonings, start with less than you think you might want. You can always add more. Too much hides the fresh natural flavors. This is particularly important when shaking Parmesan cheese on top of asparagus or a casserole before browning. All that is wanted is a little surprise flavor. The Parmesan should not dominate.

Salt I'm lost when working in a kitchen without a salt box. I keep a half-teaspoon measure in mine. I think vegetables cooked in lightly salted water have better flavor than those salted only after cooking. When making cream sauces or soups, I use salted chicken bouillon or celery salt in place of plain salt.

Sugar A little bit of sugar has a magic touch, not for making a dish sweet but to blend together the separate tastes. I learned this when trying to create the remembered flavor of a Chinese dish—I found some recipes that included sugar and this did the trick. Some meat gravies also call for a pinch of sugar. Way back, cooks used burnt sugar to darken gravies. A little sugar improves the flavor of winter squash, parsnips, turnips, and cooked tomatoes.

Onions I once read that the vegetable that would be most greatly missed if it suddenly disappeared is the onion. I agree. Onions have three flavors: pungent when raw; sweet and delicate when boiled; when lightly browned and a bit crispy—how can I describe it, a rich, pleasing flavor perhaps? Stews, meat loaves, soups—all would be flat without onion. A little coarsely chopped fresh onion added just before serving a cream soup gives a crisp, flavorful surprise. Boiled and steamed lentils and most pilafs would be too bland without browned crispy onions.

Pepper No doubt more pepper would be used if we did not

have onions. I do not cook with pepper and use it only at the table. For appearance, I like white pepper in cream sauces and soups. I do not consider pepper an essential seasoning, but one that people got used to when it was used to help preserve fresh meat before the days of refrigerators.

Lemon   A little bit of lemon juice can be transforming—it can take a greasy taste away and bring out flavor. It's well known that it improves fish, and it also makes gravies taste fresher. If you squeeze some lemon into butter and pour it on broccoli and asparagus kept refrigerated beyond their prime, you bring life back to these vegetables. But lemon's real magic is revealed when used to cook fruits. It brings out the distinctive flavors of apples, peaches, and pears.

Lemon and Orange Rind   These are as important to me for seasoning as salt and sugar. Most of us have fresh fruit around, but we do not like to mess it up by grating off the peel. I suggest saving the lemon or orange skins after using the juice. Put them in a small plastic bag in your freezer or refrigerator. When you have a fresh rind, throw out the old one.

Rinds are used mostly in baking. Add a little to any fruit pie or cobbler, but also to stewed fruit, especially prunes. For stewed fruit it does not need to be grated. The vegetable peeler is useful for shaving off pieces of rind. Also use orange rind with carrots, beets, and all kinds of winter squash.

Herbs   I had a vegetable garden for many years before I started growing any herbs other than chives and parsley. When I began growing others, it was like an adventure into the past, participating in ancient gardening, for I found herb lore to be fascinating and amusing—for example, the Greeks and Romans thought that when sowing basil seed one should curse and stamp one's feet. (I haven't tried that, but I have found that I should wait for really warm weather before planting sweet basil.)

I'm still learning about herbs. I started getting to know the flavors of a few after I became curious about herbs, and then have added one or two new ones to my herb bed each year. I would use only one herb in chicken broth until I could recognize its flavor.

Then I knew which to use to get the taste I was looking for.

Most culinary herbs need a sunny, well-drained spot in which to grow, and it is certainly handy to have it near the kitchen. Mine is above a rock wall so I can get at it from two sides. This, however, is not a good place for dill or fennel. They are too tall and like a bit more moisture and a heavier soil, so I plant them in the garden. Herbs that are fleshy, grow rapidly, and are picked frequently, such as basil and parsley, benefit from occasional fertilizing; woody-stemmed herbs, such as thyme, rosemary, and sage, do fine in ordinary soil.

Some seeds are slow in germinating. Do not let the soil get too hot or dried out. Give it a daily fine spraying of water. Herb seeds can be sown outdoors if you can keep the rain from washing them away before they sprout. Sal Gilbertie, in his book *Herb Gardening at Its Best*, suggests making miniature frame walls from half-gallon milk cartons cut in half lengthwise. He places these on the prepared outdoor seed bed and sows one kind of seed inside each frame. This way the seeds do not get washed away or mixed up.

Consider growing some of the following herbs in your garden:

Basil   Sweet basil is the kind most used in the kitchen, though you can grow ornamental purple basil (it has good flavor too) and bush basil (available from herb nurseries and good for growing indoors). Basil, an annual that blackens with the first frost, has a warm, pungent smell and a flavor that especially complements tomatoes but also almost any summer vegetable, as well as seafood. And you can blend it with garlic, olive oil, and Parmesan cheese to make pesto.

Celery Leaves   While not thought of as an herb, they can add much flavor. The older leaves have a stronger flavor than those of the heart and are a bit tough, so they should be chopped fine. Celery can be added to almost anything, and I especially like the young leaves in a salad. Chopped leaves dried are great in winter to add to soups.

Chervil   Delicate ferny leaves give a hint of chervil's uses: it goes well with delicate sauces, vegetables, and egg and cheese dishes, to which it adds a slightly licoricelike flavor. Chervil goes to seed rapidly and should be resown every few weeks for a continuous crop.

Chives I find it worthwhile to buy a clump of chives when they appear in the markets in late winter. I put it in a pot on the window sill and have fresh chives to cut. Then when the soil in the herb bed has warmed up in April, I divide the clump and plant it outside. Chives will live outside for years, but the clumps should be divided now and then. Use the purple blossoms as an edible garnish. Chives added to sour cream to serve with borscht and tomato soup are a nice touch.

Coriander This herb, also known as *Chinese parsley* or *cilantro*, has a very strong smell and robust flavor that is appreciated in Indian, Chinese, and Mexican dishes. In rich soil, the plants grow rapidly and soon bear seeds that are used in curry, pickles, and cakes.

Dill I use a lot of fresh dillweed in sauces and dips, so I make frequent plantings of dill. It usually comes rapidly from seed, but I found it would not germinate well during a spell when the nights were hot. It's a good idea to plant it in clumps if you grow a tall variety, so the wind won't blow it over. Of course, both leaves and seed heads are used in pickles, but it's good in many other dishes—with potatoes, squash, cabbage, beets, tomatoes, in dips and breads, with fish and veal.

Fennel Fennel seed comes from an herb plant. For seasoning, you can also use the feathery leaves of the vegetable Florence fennel. Fennel's anise-celery flavor complements fish especially; it is also good with cabbage and in breads. I enjoy picking off and eating the flower heads while in the garden.

Horseradish This perennial root grows easily. Freshly grated, it has a sweetly pungent, lively flavor quite unlike vinegared commercial horseradish. Grate it in the blender or food processor and use it in dips, mixed with mustard for cold cuts, or blended with butter to top vegetables.

Marjoram Similar to oregano, but milder and sweeter, marjoram must be treated as an annual in northern climates. It dries well. Use it in tomato sauces, chicken soup, or lamb dishes.

Mint Of the numerous mints, spearmint is the most familiar and versatile, but it's fun to experiment with apple mint, peppermint, orange mint, and others. Mint is good in tea, of course, and for flavoring potato salad, new peas and potatoes, cucumbers, and many Middle Eastern dishes.

Nasturtiums Not exactly an herb, but quite edible, nasturtiums have a peppery flavor that adds tang to salads or sandwiches. You can use the flowers as well as the leaves, and the seed pods can be pickled for "capers."

Oregano The "pizza herb" is wonderful in all tomato dishes. The best oregano is a hot-weather plant. Drying makes it even sweeter and more aromatic. Use it also with eggplant and mushrooms.

Parsley You can grow curly or flat-leafed parsley. A biennial, it likes rich soil. Its uses are so numerous that it should be in every garden. For flavor and color, add it to any nongreen vegetable.

Rosemary Rosemary is a beautiful semitender perennial plant, so I grow it in a large clay pot, which I remove from the herb bed before frost. I keep it over winter in a sunny window with the pot inside a ceramic container so I can water it from below. Wild rosemary grows near the Mediterranean Sea, and it gets its name from *ros marinus*, meaning dew of the sea. I find that it loves a shower bath every week when the air in the house is dry. I hold the plant on a slant over the sink and, using the spray hose, give it a good shower without also soaking the soil. Use rosemary with pickled beets, cabbage, and any kind of roast. It is excellent with game, and you can stuff a hen with rosemary sprigs before baking.

Sage Common sage is a hardy perennial herb, often associated with stuffing but also good with pork, in Cheddar cheese biscuits, in sausage, and (sparingly) in beef broth. Dry it thoroughly or it will become musty.

Savory You can grow annual summer savory or perennial winter savory, which has a stronger, more resinous flavor. Summer savory is excellent with fresh green beans, tomatoes, and stuffing for squash. Use winter savory in heartier dishes: baked beans and cold-weather soups. Steep sprigs of savory in vinegar and use it for bean salads.

Tarragon Never try to grow tarragon from seeds—it will be a kind without the lovely scent and flavor of true tarragon, which is propagated only by cuttings or root division. Once established, it is a fairly hardy perennial, though it needs some protection from cold in winter and rabbits in the spring. A frame made from a large plastic bottle does the job. Cut the top and bottom off. Use tarragon with almost any vegetable, chicken, veal, and seafood. Vinegar flavored with tarragon is especially good on home-grown lettuce salads.

Thyme Many kinds of thyme can be grown; most are hardy perennials with a pungent smell and taste that is good with vegetables—squash, onions, eggplant—and in stuffings, clam chowder, and beef stock.

Some herbs are complementary, such as chives, parsley, a little onion, and also fresh peppers, and may be used with other herbs, but I do not recommend just any old mixture. It's much more pleasant to taste the distinctive flavors of rosemary, tarragon, and basil. There are three instances when I do sometimes mix herb flavors: in salads, in dips, and in vegetable soups. (I must admit that I have found one commercial mixture I like very much, McCormick's Salad Herbs, in which you already have mixed-up flavors.) For information on drying and freezing herbs see page 197.

Fresh Peppers Though peppers are not classified as an herb or a spice, they are often used to add flavor and color. Their flavor does not mask others, so I often add them to soups and sauces or even golden beans and summer squash. The flavor diffuses through things better when the pepper is peeled, which I do quite easily with my swivel peeler.

I did not become acquainted with hot fresh peppers in the

kitchen until Indian dishes were prepared there. The Indians like things hot and highly seasoned. I once put a bit of hot red pepper in a squash casserole by mistake and was delighted with the result. So I have cautiously used a little fresh hot pepper in soups and dips and found that it adds a more pleasant flavor than ordinary ground pepper.

Spices   These are used primarily with winter vegetables: nutmeg or allspice with mashed winter squash; cinnamon and nutmeg with baked candied squash and parsnips; fresh ginger with cauliflower and cabbage; and combinations of allspice, cloves, ginger, brown sugar, and vinegar when making sweet-and-sour sauces for red cabbage and beets. Saffron, a very delicate and expensive seasoning, is used primarily with rice. Real saffron is the stigma of a crocus. Gardeners can harvest a substitute, "poor man's saffron," simply by growing marigolds.

Seeds   The use of seeds for flavoring is common in India. Cumin and coriander seeds are used with stir-fried vegetables. Sesame seeds are used in baking and with specific vegetables, such as eggplant. I think of seeds as having a nutty taste.

Nuts   These are seeds, too, and the use of slivered almonds with green beans and fish is common. It is the contrast in texture as well as their flavor that I enjoy. Water chestnuts, which really are tubers, are a pleasant addition to Chinese foods, primarily because of their crunch. Pine nuts, or pignoli, have a delightful diffusive

---

Poor Man's Saffron Rice

Pull petals from center of golden or orange marigolds until you have about ¼ cup lightly packed petals. Put petals on a cutting board and with a sharp knife cut them into shreds. Add them to 2½ cups boiling water, 1 cup rice, and ½ teaspoon salt. Return to a boil and then lower heat and cook for 20 minutes. Drain and season with butter. For more flavorful rice use chicken stock in place of water.

flavor when lightly browned. They are a good addition to white rice, and the Arabs in Tiberias make a festive main dish of pounded meat and bulgur layered with pine nuts and onions.

Sauces These are a way of conveying a flavor—subtle or strong—to the dish they accompany.

White sauces are usually subtle, but they don't have to be bland or boring. I use herb-flavored chicken stock for some of the liquid, or add a complementary flavoring, such as parsley, chives, chervil, dill, or fresh peppers.

○ *Basic White Sauce*

A creamier sauce than this can be made by using undiluted evaporated milk in place of the powdered milk and regular milk.

4 tablespoons flour
⅓ cup powdered milk to make
  sauce whiter and richer in flavor
1-2 tablespoons butter, depending
  on fat in stock

1 cup fresh milk
1 cup seasoned hot chicken stock
½ teaspoon instant chicken
  bouillon crystals, optional

Mix flour and powdered milk together. Melt the butter in a heavy pot or the top of a double boiler over boiling water. Stir in the flour mixture, then slowly pour in the cold milk, stirring constantly. Add the hot chicken stock and stir until thickened and smooth. Taste before adding the broth crystals. Do not cover the sauce or it will get runny.   *Makes 2 cups.*

Now you have your basic sauce and you can add color and flavoring with an herb or finely chopped peppers. You might like a shake or two of white pepper. Or you can stir in grated cheese.

Sweet-and-Sour Sauces These are distinctive and make a vegetable taste quite different. I like a sweet-and-sour sauce with red vegetables because it seems to brighten the color. You can have fun with spices and use small amounts until you get the flavor you are searching for. The basic sauce is made with cornstarch for thickener, using 1 tablespoon to 1 cup of the liquor in which the vegetable was cooked. For a strong sour flavor, use 3 tablespoons white vinegar and 1 tablespoon brown sugar. Add 1 tablespoon butter and salt to taste. Add allspice, cloves, or ginger as an artist adds color.

I realize I have not mentioned garlic. It is not a flavor found in Arabic cooking and therefore was not one I'd encountered in my youth. I like a hint of it now and then with roast lamb, a green salad, or some stir-fried dishes when it is used to season the oil, but basically I seldom use it because it can be overpowering.

I am not a purist when it comes to cooking, so I do use commercial seasonings and have on a shelf near the stove celery salt and a pleasantly seasoned salt called Jane's Krazy Mixed-up Salt to use when I am in a hurry and a sauce or dip needs a lift. I use canned soups, but I add a touch of my own—leftover green vegetable, diced onion, parsley, or chives.

Seasoning choices are all a matter of your own memories and personal tastes. Do not hesitate to make changes in recipes when you know a flavor you wish to use. This is where you really can be creative and give food your own distinctive touch. It makes cooking much more fun.

5
Early
Vegetables

PARKER LEIGHTON

After eating frozen vegetables and store produce through the harsh winter months and erratic March, I long for fresh vegetables from the garden. The first ones taste so much sweeter. In eastern Pennsylvania it is traditional to plant peas on St. Patrick's Day and onion sets for scallions in March also, but I think this is rushing the season. It is best to wait until the earth has dried out a bit and started to warm up.

The first asparagus of the season tastes better than anything else I grow because it is the first fresh crop of the year.

Asparagus comes up before you know it. As soon as the ground has thawed in the spring, I go to my asparagus patch and look for those first shoots. I learned from my grandfather that when you harvest asparagus (except for the first spears) you should make sure there's another sprout coming up from the hill before you pick one. This assures that you won't starve the plant's roots.

Although I do not recommend asparagus for a small garden, you can get quite a nice supply from a twenty-five-foot row if you plant the hills a foot apart, and it's one of the best gardening investments you can make, since a bed will bear for many years. The roots should be placed in a trench with manure and good topsoil in early spring. (You can also plant seeds, but you'll have to wait longer to harvest a good crop.) Gradually fill in the trench with rich soil as the plants grow. Additions of fertilizer, one in March and another in July, increase productivity in following years.

Asparagus is a challenging and rewarding vegetable to grow. But it needs patience just as much as good soil and sun. I recommend waiting at least three years for the first harvest from roots to allow your plants to establish themselves. One of the nice things about waiting is that you'll have a beautiful fernlike hedge during the summer—there is nothing quite like asparagus foliage to use in flower arrangements.

Weeds grow readily in the rich soil of an asparagus bed, but in order not to damage the plants you should not use a hoe. I make sure my asparagus bed is continually mulched right from the start, and I find that well-decayed leaves are the best mulch.

Asparagus foliage should be cut off in the fall so no stalks are left standing through winter. This leaves the crowns of the plants open for development of new buds in spring. It also destroys any asparagus beetles, which hibernate in the stems of old plants.

In spring I pull out any very skinny young seedlings that appear, especially those that develop in the crowns. Some people cut off all female stalks as soon as their berries appear. This helps the roots to develop strength and prevents more seedlings from coming up.

Green or purplish-green garden asparagus (such as Mary Washington) is not the same variety as the white kind sold in cans. White asparagus is blanched and generally comes up through straw. (At one time it was considered more "elite" to serve white asparagus, and it is still preferred by many Europeans.) You can blanch your asparagus by using an extra amount of lightly packed mulch around the stalks, but doing this reduces both the food value and the flavor.

I prefer to break asparagus spears off rather than cut them at the soil with a knife. A knife might cut a spear still under the surface, and by breaking I bring in only the tender part of the spear. Asparagus sold in stores usually has six inches of tough white stem, and I suggest that the white ends be snapped off rather than cut, so what you serve will be entirely edible. The green part has the most flavor. Of course, you can peel the tough skin off the white part and use it for soup.

○ *Boiled Asparagus*

There is no need to peel tender spears. I lay the stalks flat, not more than two layers and all pointing the same way, in a flat pan or skillet, and pour boiling water over them to barely cover. Do not cover pan. Let water boil, and test after 5 minutes. I lift a stalk out and hold it horizontal. When it bends, the asparagus is done. It may take longer, depending on the thickness and age of the stalks. Drain the water off, holding the pan so that the stalks are horizontal. Put back on a warm burner and add butter and salt to taste. Then roll asparagus onto a serving dish.

° Stir-Fried Asparagus

Cut the stalks at an angle into 1½-inch-long pieces. Heat just enough oil to cover the bottom of a flat pan or wok. Add asparagus and stir-fry for 5–6 minutes, until bright green. The asparagus should still be firm. It needs only salt for seasoning, but you can shake a little Parmesan cheese on top.

° Steamed Asparagus

I do not steam asparagus, but if you want to, tie up stalks in bundles and place bottoms down in a tall pot (or in the bottom of a double boiler with the top inverted), with 2 inches of boiling water in the bottom. Or place on a steam rack. Cover and steam for 8–10 minutes.

Other Ideas for Asparagus

- I like to serve asparagus with fish or a cheese soufflé or macaroni and cheese—not with highly seasoned meats.
- Serve pencil-thin very fresh raw asparagus spears with a dip.
- Make cream of asparagus soup: Reserving tips, purée cooked asparagus in blender with some cooking liquid. Add cream, lemon juice, and herbs to taste. Decorate with asparagus tips.
- Serve cold cooked asparagus with a horseradish–sour cream sauce, or a mustard vinaigrette, or herbed mayonnaise. Sprinkle with chopped hard-boiled eggs.
- Wrap prosciutto or Westphalian ham around small bundles of asparagus. Serve hot or cold.
- Parboil asparagus 4 minutes, dip in beaten egg, then Parmesan cheese and fresh bread crumbs, and sauté in butter and oliver oil.
- Asparagus is wonderful with eggs: add parboiled chopped spears to a frittata, soufflé, quiche, omelet, or to scrambled eggs.

Garden cress is one of the quickest crops you can grow from seed. I was introduced to it as a child, when we kept cress growing on absorbent cotton in a dish of water set in the center of our dining-room table. We snipped off the young greens when they were about 1½ inches tall.

Outdoors, I start planting garden cress in very early spring. It's nice to have it on hand to use as a garnish before parsley is available—cress is ready to eat just ten days after planting. I also sow seeds around September 1, and I enjoy this crop even more. In fall, cress grows a little more slowly and the texture of the leaves is firmer. It needs to be protected when a frost is predicted.

When I learned from a friend that containers of cress growing on cocofiber mat are sold in Dutch and Scandinavian markets, I wondered what I might have that was like cocofiber. I wanted to take cress to a garden-club meeting. I shook the dirt out of an old doormat and ran hot water over it until I thought it could be called clean. I put foil on a large tray and the soaking door mat on that. Then I sprinkled the cress seeds on the mat and rubbed my hands over it to press the seeds into it. I watered the mat so that the seeds would all get wet, covered it with wax paper, and put it in a warm place. In three days the young plants could be seen, and I put the tray in a sunny window and removed the wax paper. I watered the mat each day, and in two weeks I had a lovely miniature jungle, which I took to the club meeting. The mat slid off the tray as I carried it in, but no harm was done—it landed rooted side down. We all had a great time snipping away at the cress forest.

I am very fond of using Curlycress (Burpee's brand of garden cress) with cold meats and in salads. The peppery flavor is also delicious in bread-and-butter sandwiches, a popular use in Europe. I prefer to make just cress and lettuce salads with nothing else added except a light oil-and-vinegar dressing. Everything extra masks the cress flavor. When using garden cress, add one-fourth the volume of lettuce you have broken up. Curlycress can also be used for sprouts.

Watercress, though a sturdier plant than garden cress, has a milder flavor. It will grow very easily in any wet place with flowing water. The seed can be started in a seed-starting container which has been set in a pan of water so that the soil stays constantly moist. When the plants are one or two inches tall, just set the container in a stream or pond with moving water, close to the bank so you can reach it. Watercress has both a spring and a fall season; cut it back after each season of growth. It also resows itself.

When adding watercress to salads, use one-third cress and two-thirds lettuce. Watercress has enough body to be served alone too. In this case a blue-cheese dressing made with oil and vinegar, not creamy, is good. Some bacon bits or croutons may be added.

Most home gardeners like to boast about their first pickings from the garden, and like them I look forward to serving a garden lettuce salad. The earliest lettuces to be ready to use are the loosehead types, which can be picked in only forty-five days—some sooner when I thin out the little plants and use them.

Most loose-leaf lettuces are good only in late spring and early summer because as soon as the weather gets warm they bolt—the center stalk shoots up to produce blooms. I let what I haven't used in time bolt because I learned from Arab women to eat the succulent inner core of the stem. It can be a substitute for celery or cut as cucumber in a salad.

Lettuce can be started indoors when you want to rush the garden season, but it is not necessary to do so unless the slower-growing crisp-head types are your favorites. I don't get the same kind of kick out of sowing seeds indoors as I do in the garden. There is something soothing about being outside in the sun and breaking lumps of soil in a furrow with my hands before planting seeds, then spreading the thin layer of soil over them and patting it down.

Undoubtedly the seedlings will come up thicker than for proper spacing for good plant development. You can eat young lettuce when it is 2½–3 inches tall by making use of the plants you thin out. Cut them off at the soil line with a knife. This does not disturb the soil around the roots of the plants left behind, and the lettuce you bring in will be cleaner.

Because there are individual flavors and textures to each type of lettuce, I grow several kinds. You can choose from the following:

Loosehead Lettuces, including Black-Seeded Simpson, are the quickest to grow to edible size, are soft in texture, and need tender care in handling. These should be picked in the cool of morning.

Speeding Germination

If you are an impatient gardener, you may want to water well with a fine nozzle right after planting and keep the soil moist until seedlings appear. A trick I have used is to put a flat board over the seeded row and keep it there for three days. Then I raise one side up so air can get under it. The board keeps the soil moist and also keeps my dog from trampling on the planted row. (I need the dog to keep the rabbits away.)

Fordhook and Green Ice are medium loosehead varieties that have good color, firm texture, and a pronounced flavor. They can be used for salads that one wants to keep crisp for quite a while on a buffet (as is the ubiquitous iceberg, of course, which has very little flavor compared to other lettuces).

Oak Leaf and Salad Bowl are reliable loosehead lettuce varieties for hot seasons. However, they have comparatively small leaves of very soft texture. Royal Oak Leaf is greener and firmer.

Butterhead Lettuces—Bibb, Buttercrunch, and Boston—are ideal when you are serving individual salads. They make the prettiest lettuce cups, as the leaves separate from the head easily and can be cut with a salad fork. Unfortunately, they grow well only in cool seasons.

Romaine or Cos Lettuce has elongated, firm-textured leaves and crunchy midribs that are delicious in Caesar salad or tossed with other greens.

Endive, which is slightly pungent, comes with fringed leaves (sometimes called chicory) or broad leaves (escarole). It is not a lettuce but a lettuce substitute.

Lettuce from the garden is best picked in the morning when the leaves are crisp. Wash it right away by dipping the whole head up and down in water or letting water flow among the leaves. Turn it upside down to drip dry; shaking helps.

When lettuce is brought home from the market, unwrap it and put it in the hydrator of your refrigerator. If loosehead types are a bit wilted, dunk the head a few times in cold water. Put it stem end up in your drainage rack for ten minutes or more before refrigerating.

If you prepare lettuce ahead of time, put it on a hand towel or clean dish towel, fold this over the lettuce, and put it in the refrigerator until you are ready to mix the salad.

The secret of a good tossed green salad is dry, crisp greens carefully handled. If greens are wet, an oil dressing will run off them and end up at the bottom of the bowl. If they are twisted or chopped, the flavor and texture will be destroyed. I object strongly to lettuce cut with a kitchen knife. It changes the flavor and produces unexpected long strips of lettuce that hang from a fork like green hay. Pieces should not be larger than the average open mouth. Tear each leaf apart with your fingers into mouth-size pieces that are easy to pick up with a fork. The cook should always think of how a person is to get what's on his plate to his mouth in an attractive manner.

○ *Lettuce Salads*

Use more than one type of lettuce, or use the heart leaves of one and the green outside leaves of another. Escarole, endive, watercress, or young spinach leaves can be substituted for one type of lettuce, but I prefer they not be more than one-third of the total greens. Any of the following go into my tossed salads:

Fresh Ripe Tomatoes   The skins can be loosened quickly by gently running a dull knife over the entire surface; then start peeling from the blossom end. Or they can be dipped briefly in boiling water to loosen the peel. Cut the tomato into bite-size sections and put them on a plate until ready to use. Then lift the sections off the plate, discarding the juice and seedy parts that slip out.

Tomato Aspic   I use this when vine-ripened tomatoes are not available. Cut the aspic into one-inch cubes and mix in the salad bowl. (See page 132 for recipe.)

Celery   Add the young light-green leaves of one of the stalks from the heart of the celery bunch. Cut the leaves with kitchen scissors. Also, string a single stalk of celery and cut it across into quarter-inch widths for extra crispness.

Onion   Salads can be ruined by too much onion. Use only two thin slices for a bowl of lettuce to serve two or three. Cut the slices into thirds and separate them into crescents. The pieces should be large enough to be seen. (When I use turnip, radish, watercress, or kohlrabi in salads, I do not add onion.)

Parsley   Cut with scissors and use about two tablespoons of fresh parsley for a salad bowl for four. Experiment with other herbs—snipped chives, savory, dill, basil—but not all at the same time.

Marinated Cooked Vegetables   Especially in the winter when I do not have fresh tomatoes, I save leftover vegetables just for salads in one container in the refrigerator. (I always put broccoli in a separate container, for its flavor permeates the other vegetables.)

Root vegetables can be marinated in salad dressing for quite a long time, but green vegetables for only five or ten minutes because they will lose their firmness and green color.

Green beans are especially good with lettuce that has little body because they give substance to the salad. Don't marinate them for long or their color will change. Just mix them with a bit of the salad dressing and add to the salad bowl just before serving.

Asparagus should be cut into one-inch lengths with kitchen scissors. It is good raw or cooked in salads.

Broccoli and cauliflower have a dominant flavor, so I use them separately, not with a mixture of other vegetables.

Sprouts   The addition of home-grown sprouts of any kind adds interest to a lettuce salad. Alfalfa sprouts are our favorite, but mustard sprouts add more zest to the salad. It is fun to grow them in wide jars with perforated lids, especially in winter. Mung beans are the

---

A Tip for Pickle Juice

Keep all your leftover pickle juices—it's okay to mix them—as they are good for marinating. I use them as an ingredient in salad dressing, for preparing Harvard beets, and even for basting fish, broiled ham, and barbecued meats. In sweet-and-sour dishes I use pickle juice with brown sugar added, tasting until I get the flavor I want.

most common seed used for sprouting, but I think they lack flavor even though the sprouts are larger.

Other things to be added when available, but not all of them at one time:

Cucumber, peeled and sliced.
Young kohlrabi, peeled and sliced.
Turnip, peeled and sliced.
Radishes, sliced.
Young zucchini, sliced.
Pickles. Substitute these for tomatoes in a plain lettuce salad when you have no tomatoes to use.

○*Grapefruit and Orange Salad*

This was the first salad our son ever ate and is still his favorite. In late spring when lettuce is plentiful but the summer vegetables to add to a mixed salad are not yet available, I add a 16-ounce can of mixed grapefruit and orange sections to a 10-inch bowl full of bits of lettuce of different types. As I am never without celery, I add some cut-up celery leaves. I use the juice from the mixed fruit half and half with Old-Fashioned French Dressing (following recipe) and serve with cottage cheese. Canned pears may be substituted for the grapefruit and orange.

○*Dressings for Salads*

OLD-FASHIONED FRENCH DRESSING

⅓ cup cider vinegar or herbed wine vinegar
½ teaspoon celery salt
⅛ teaspoon white pepper or 2 drops Tabasco

1 teaspoon onion juice or finely grated onion
⅛ teaspoon paprika
1 teaspoon sugar
¾ cup vegetable or olive oil

Shake together all ingredients except oil until well mixed. Add oil and shake vigorously before serving. **Approx. 1¼ cups.**

GRANDMOTHER'S BOILED OIL DRESSING

This is especially good with a salad of tomatoes, cucumber, and watercress.

2 tablespoons flour	½ cup water or milk
1 teaspoon dry mustard	½ tablespoon butter
1 teaspoon salt	1 egg yolk
1 tablespoon sugar	½ cup vegetable oil
A good pinch of cayenne pepper or ⅛ teaspoon white pepper	3 tablespoons cider vinegar mixed with 1 tablespoon water

Mix together the flour, mustard, salt, sugar, and pepper. Slowly add water or milk (milk makes the dressing creamier) and mix well. Melt butter in the top of a double boiler, add flour mixture, and cook over almost boiling water, stirring vigorously. It thickens fast. Beat egg yolk with vegetable oil. Add slowly to the flour mixture while beating with an egg beater or a whisk. Add mixture of cider vinegar and 1 tablespoon water slowly and beat while cooking about 3 minutes more. *Approx. 1½ cups.*

VINEGAR-AND-SUGAR DRESSING

Pour a little cider vinegar on young loosehead garden lettuce leaves and sprinkle with granulated sugar. This was Grandpa's favorite.

DOYLESTOWN DRESSING (AUNT MYRTLE'S RECIPE)

This is a type of Russian dressing, good for firm-textured lettuces.

1 slice Bermuda onion about 1 inch thick	½ cup ketchup
2 tablespoons brown sugar	1 tablespoon A-1 or Worcestershire sauce
2 tablespoons lemon juice	¼ cup olive oil

Mix all together in the blender or food processor. *Makes about 1 cup.*

Other Ideas for Lettuce

- Wild greens can add flavor and surprise to lettuce salads—try purslane, young dandelion leaves, field cress, steamed fiddlehead ferns, sorrel, lamb's-quarters.
- Add a flower garnish to the salad bowl—marigold petals, nasturtium flowers and leaves, rose petals, and violets are all edible.
- Make a lettuce soup to serve hot or cold by simmering chopped lettuce in chicken stock, adding light cream and seasoning to taste.
- Stuff lettuce leaves as you would grape or cabbage leaves: blanch large, firm lettuce leaves, roll them around your favorite stuffing, and braise in broth.
- Cook a few lettuce leaves with young peas to add moisture and a subtle flavor.
- Braise shredded lettuce to serve as a side dish. Small plump lettuces may be braised whole.
- Leftover lettuce salad, even if dressed with oil and vinegar, can be blended into gazpacho.

Celtuce, a type of lettuce grown and eaten commonly in the Orient, was introduced to American gardeners by the Burpee Seed Company and was given its name because it combines the uses of both lettuce and celery. The leaves are long like romaine lettuce and high in vitamin C. The center stalk, which is at least an inch thick, grows to eighteen inches tall, but the plants are at their best at twelve to fourteen inches.

Celtuce is planted in the garden as soon as danger of frost is over. It is important not to crowd the plants so that the stalks will be thick.

The leaves of celtuce are slightly bitter. They are picked singly from the stalk and can be used raw in salad or steamed. The choice part of the plant is the succulent light-green center of the stalks. Raw celtuce hearts are excellent for nibbling or adding to salads as a substitute for cucumber. Use an herb-seasoned salt on them when serving as finger food. Or they can be cooked like celery.

∘ Chinese-Style Celtuce Stalks

Peel and discard the outer skin of the celtuce stalks and slice the hearts. Cook in a meat broth with small pieces of meat, flavoring it with onion, ginger, and peppers. Thicken the broth slightly with cornstarch and serve with soy sauce on the side.

○*Celtuce Leaves with Bacon Dressing*

4 strips bacon	¼ teaspoon salt
1 tablespoon flour	¼ teaspoon pepper
1 tablespoon sugar	1-2 tablespoons vinegar
1 egg	4 cups washed, dried, cut-up
1 cup milk	celtuce leaves

Fry bacon and drain, leaving fat in the pan. Mix flour and sugar, add egg, and beat well. Stir in milk. Put in pan containing fat and bring to a boil, stirring constantly. Season with salt, pepper, and vinegar. Add the celtuce leaves. Serve as soon as celtuce has become warm. Crumble bacon on top. **Serves 2-3.**

Variation: Substitute escarole or Romano beans for the celtuce.

○*Celtuce au Gratin*

This is very good as part of a vegetarian meal (but not with beets or tomatoes).

1 cup celtuce, peeled and cut into	1 cup milk or light cream
1-inch slices	¼ teaspoon salt
2 tablespoons butter	½ cup grated Cheddar cheese
1½ tablespoons flour	

Boil celtuce in a small amount of water until tender. Meanwhile, make a light cream sauce: melt the butter in a small heavy pot, stir in the flour until blended, then stir in milk or cream until smooth. Season with salt. Mix half the grated cheese into the sauce, add to drained celtuce, and mix. Put into a buttered baking dish. Sprinkle remaining cheese on top. Heat under the broiler until top is brown.

Serves 1.

○ *Creamed Celtuce*

Peel celtuce stalks and cut across or in strips to make about 3 cups. Boil in water just to cover until tender, about 15 minutes, and drain. Make Basic White Sauce, page 30. Mix sauce, celtuce stems, and ⅓ cup finely chopped young celtuce leaves, and place in a buttered casserole. Sprinkle grated cheese or seasoned bread crumbs on top and bake in a 300° oven for 10–15 minutes or until brown on top. This dish goes well with broiled fish.   *Serves 3.*

An eastern Mediterranean vegetable belonging to the cabbage family, kohlrabi has a delicate cabbagy flavor that deserves to be enjoyed a lot more than it is. It thrives in cool weather and, like others of the cabbage family, seems to have better flavor after frost—try a late planting this season for a pleasant surprise. I plant one crop in spring and another toward the end of the gardening season. It will mature just before frost, and can be ready for use 45 days from the time seed is sown.

Sow the seeds directly in the garden. When the seedlings are up, thin the plants to about five inches apart by pulling out the extra seedlings and transplanting them. Because the transplants grow more slowly than the ones left in place, your harvest is extended.

The leaves are edible, but kohlrabi is mainly grown for the large bulbous stem that develops an inch above ground level. It can be picked as soon as it is 1½ inches across. Because it is a stem, the most tender and tasty part is at the tip and just under the skin. The skin is tough and should be peeled off carefully. There are purple and white varieties, but the color is only skin deep.

The bulbs become woody and fibrous if left too long in the garden, especially in warm weather, so it's best to pick them at their peak and store them in the refrigerator rather than let them grow too large. They will keep at least a month refrigerated. Some of the newer varieties, such as Grand Duke hybrid, grow large quickly, stay more tender, and have less fiber in the center than the older varieties.

My family prefer kohlrabi raw, but creamed kohlrabi is excellent with fish or cold chicken or turkey, as its flavor is mild. When making creamed kohlrabi, dice the kohlrabi and cook in just enough water to cover. Save this water after cooking to use half and half with milk in preparing a cream sauce with a kohlrabi flavor.

Other Ideas for Kohlrabi

- Slices of kohlrabi are excellent to use in place of chips when serving a creamy herb-seasoned dip. Crisp the slices in the refrigerator in very lightly salted water.
- Grate raw kohlrabi with carrots, red sweet peppers, and lots of parsley for an unusual coleslaw.
- Use kohlrabi as a substitute in recipes calling for radishes or turnips.
- Cook small whole kohlrabies and their greens separately until tender, then toss together with butter.
- Grate kohlrabi and carrots, stir-fry or steam them until tender, and use as a garnish or a side dish.

As I look through a seed catalog to select the varieties to list on my order, my mouth waters in anticipation of the pleasure of plucking a first pea pod from the vine and eating the peas raw.

Peas are the first seeds planted in my garden—the vines grow best when it is cool, and they will not flower in hot weather. I choose the early and shorter varieties that will grow without support, but if I lived where the weather is cooler, I would certainly select varieties that grow two feet or taller, for they are easier on the back to pick, and they bear longer.

Peas are one of the few garden plants that produce some of their needed nutrients from nodules that grow on their roots, so they should not be generously fertilized or they will grow and grow and grow and not bloom. In order to keep the vines off the ground, I plant the seeds in two rows eight inches apart. Then the vines help to hold one another up and it is easier to see the pods when picking.

For ordinary green peas, it is best to let the pods fill out so that the peas inside are round. Very young peas are watery and have not developed their sweetness. But this sweetness goes as soon as a pod loses its smooth surface.

Edible-podded peas, as their name suggests, are varieties of peas which have sweet, crisp, but tender pods that lose their sweetness as the peas develop inside. They are variously known as sugar peas, snow peas, or China peas (since they are popular in Oriental cooking). These peas should be eaten while the pods are still succulent, but if you miss some you can still shell and eat the peas before they get too large. Some need a support to cling to as they grow. You can stretch string between posts or, better, buy the string-and-plastic trellises now available at garden centers.

Sugar Snap, a new but already popular edible-podded pea, is the forerunner of a new class of peas, ones that have sweet, fleshy pods that retain their sweetness even when full of peas inside. The vines grow very tall, over six feet, and it takes seventy days until the first pods appear, but they are worth waiting for and are eaten raw as often as cooked. I have wound a piece of string trellis around an old, tall, dome-shaped jungle gym to support my Sugar Snap peas. Of course, I left an opening so I could get inside to pick. This has worked well for me, though unfortunately it is not big enough for all the peas I would like—snap peas are also good when frozen, so it's hard to get enough for eating raw, cooking, *and* freezing.

In order to get the most from the garden, it is important how peas are picked. Do not send your youngsters out to do it unless you have taught them how. Pea vines do not have a lot of roots, so they are easily pulled up, and the pods are very firmly attached to the vine and cannot be yanked off. One hand should hold the vine below the pod and the other pull the pod off. It is best to pick peas every two or three days because on warm days they mature quickly, especially the edible-podded type. Whenever I go to my garden, I walk by these vines and gather the pods (they keep well in the refrigerator, dry, in plastic bags). After any peas are brought to the house, keep them cool. If you are not going to use them the same day, shell them (unless edible-podded) and refrigerate in a closed container.

Because peas are shallow-rooted, do not weed or scratch the soil around them. If you are a meticulous gardener, put a layer of dry mulch around the peas when they are at least six inches tall, or cut the weeds at the soil line as they grow. I am usually too busy to keep after all the weeds, so some do grow around the peas and help to hold them up, but I do not let the weeds go to seed.

Cook peas uncovered in boiling water only until they have softened and lost their raw taste. The skins come off if they are overcooked. I don't think they need salt. If peas are beyond their sweetest stage, add two or three washed lettuce leaves to the water. Drain the peas, but they should be served slightly moist with butter or cream.

◦ Grandpa's Favorite Spring Dish

Cook 2 cups fresh peas, 2 cups baby carrots, and a 2-inch strip of unsmoked salt pork together in water to cover. Serve in the liquor and eat with bread and butter.

◦ Sugar Snap Peas

Unlike that of snow peas, the flavor of snap peas is best when the peas have formed inside the pod. Remove the string on the straight edge, then snap the pod in half and cook pod and peas as you would ordinary peas—that is, if you haven't eaten them all raw first. Do not overcook them—a couple of minutes is enough—or they will lose flavor and fall apart. You can also batter-fry them as tempura, add them to stews just before serving, or pickle them as you would green beans.

◦ Snow Peas and Water Chestnuts

Snow peas are sweetest before the peas inside are conspicuous. They also have a bit of a string on the straight edge that should be removed. When the peas wilt, which they do very quickly, I think they lose some of their sweetness.

These peas are especially good with other Chinese dishes, but they can be served with anything. Serve with soy sauce on the side. If you don't have water chestnuts, you may substitute celery.

½ pound snow peas
1 tablespoon oil
½ cup thinly sliced water
chestnuts

1 cup chicken stock
1 tablespoon cornstarch dissolved
in 2 tablespoons cold chicken
stock

Snap off the ends of the peas and pull back to remove strings. Heat the oil in a skillet or wok. Add peas and water chestnuts and toss to coat. Add the cup of stock, bring to a boil, then cover and cook over high heat for 3 minutes. Push vegetables to one side and add mixture of cornstarch and stock to the liquid in the pan. Stir only until slightly thickened, then mix vegetables in.   **Serves 2-3.**

Other Ideas for Peas

- Good herbs for use with peas are mint, marjoram, basil, and dill. A little nutmeg is also nice.
- Peas go well mixed with lightly sautéed fresh white mushrooms and pearl onions, and they are the perfect accompaniment to tiny new potatoes.
- Make spring green-pea soup: Cook peas in chicken stock until tender, purée in a food mill, and stir in cream. Season with salt and pepper, chopped mint, or curry powder. Add diced cooked chicken meat if you like. See also Chicken Broth and Puréed Green Peas, page 217.
- Stir-fry snow peas or snap peas with shrimp and serve hot with rice. Or toss cooked peas, shrimp, and rice with vinaigrette and chill for a salad.
- Add leftover cooked peas to potato salad or mixed vegetable salads.
- Purée cooked peas and fold them into mashed potatoes to make them a lovely green color.
- Don't discard green peas past their prime; cook them until tender, purée, and add to meat loaf or use to thicken sauces.

Popeye the Sailor Man gave cooked spinach a great popularity boost in the late thirties. I do not know who started serving raw spinach salad, but that use has kept it in the front-runner ranks.

Unfortunately, spinach is one of those plants that is in a hurry to produce seed as soon as the weather gets in the upper seventies, so it must be planted in the garden as soon as the soil has dried out and warmed up to above 40°F. It is also possible to have a fall crop of spinach if planted in September in mid-Atlantic states. The variety Winter Bloomsdale will live through the winter for early spring use. Cover seeds with a half inch of fine soil, and thin seedlings (use them in salad) to five or six inches apart. Spinach plants need room to spread out; otherwise they grow tall and spindly. Water the seeds as they will not germinate unless the soil is wet. After that spinach does not need a lot of water, but it will appreciate some fertilizer.

Spinach is usually ready to pick in about forty-five days from seed planting. Take a knife to the garden and cut the entire plant off a half inch above the soil; this makes it easier to clean. Dump the spinach into a sink full of water, swish it around, and remove the spinach. Then drain the water out of the sink and get rid of the grit. Do this over again until there is no grit on the bottom of the sink. If you drain the water with the spinach in the sink, the grit goes back into it.

I'm not an advocate of steaming spinach because the cooking is uneven and the resulting flavor too strong for my taste. Instead, put washed spinach in a pot (if doing a large quantity, use a spaghetti cooker or blancher) and pour boiling water over it to almost cover. Add a teaspoon of salt. Bring rapidly to a boil uncovered, turning the spinach over frequently. The cooking time depends on the age of the spinach and the quantity; it could be done in five minutes. Taste. When done, empty into a colander and flip it over several times to get water out, or press down on it with a spoon. Chop it in the colander and leave in colander over steam until ready to serve. Season the spinach in the serving dish.

Spinach has so much flavor I add only butter, but if you wish, add a little finely chopped raw onion, or condensed cream of mushroom soup right out of the can, in place of butter (in this case, do not add salt when cooking). Or use your own thick cream sauce. Some people like vinegar on spinach.

Spinach can be served with any meat, fish, or cheese dish. See also discussions elsewhere of Malabar spinach, New Zealand spinach, and tampala.

∘ *Spinach and Zucchini*

The last of my spinach and the first zucchini usually coincide, and that is when I prepare this dish. The pieces of celery and scallion should be smaller than the zucchini pieces.

1 zucchini, 1½ inches in diameter	½ cup Basic White Sauce (see page 30)
1 cup chopped cooked spinach	
½ cup parboiled scallions cut into ¼-inch lengths	2 tablespoons seasoned bread crumbs
½ cup parboiled diced celery	1 tablespoon grated Parmesan cheese
	½ tablespoon butter

Parboil the zucchini whole, then quarter it lengthwise and cut quarters into halves. Mix together zucchini, spinach, scallions, and celery with white sauce in a double boiler and heat until warm. Turn into a flat baking dish, sprinkle seasoned bread crumbs and Parmesan cheese on top, and dot with butter. Put under the broiler for a few minutes. **Serves 4.**

° *Spinach Salad*

Often spinach is used alone with dressing and other seasonings in salads, but I prefer a combination of half spinach and half green loosehead lettuce—romaine, Fordhook, or Green Ice. I think spinach salad calls for bits of something with a strong flavor to be mixed with it, such as crumbled bacon or cut-up green olives, an oil-and-vinegar dressing, and salad croutons.

Other Ideas for Spinach

- ° Many herbs go well with spinach. Try basil, dill, oregano, or tarragon.
- ° For cream of spinach soup, good hot or cold, purée chopped cooked spinach in a food mill, then stir in cream. For a thicker, richer soup, beat in 2 egg yolks. You can also add bits of ham or chicken.
- ° Use spinach in soufflés, timbales, quiches, omelets, crêpes.
- ° When making lasagne, add a layer or two of chopped spinach mixed with ricotta cheese and eggs. Or use spinach as a layer in pâtés.
- ° Make a beautiful rice ring by combining 1 cup chopped cooked spinach, 3 cups cooked rice, 2 eggs, and 1 cup cream. Bake in a greased ring mold at 325°F. for 30 minutes, then unmold and fill center with creamed mushrooms or chicken or a colorful vegetable.
- ° A green dip or sauce is easily made by combining finely chopped spinach, parsley, and garlic with mayonnaise and/or sour cream.
- ° Use puréed spinach as a bed for baked eggs, poached chicken breasts, or croquettes.

Radish seeds are the best to use to stimulate a child's interest in gardening, for they are easy to sow, they can be planted early (radishes thrive in cool weather), and harvest is quick—less than a month. If you are having a child sow the seeds, I suggest that you mix them with sand, twice as much sand as seeds, and scatter the mixture in the row, for it is most important that radishes not be crowded. When you think of the size of the radish you expect to pull, you will not sow the seeds too thick. Cover them with about a half inch of soil.

The flavor of the varieties of radish does not vary as much as the shape, and there are white and black ones as well as the familiar red. The whites are apt to be sweeter. Some varieties grow long and stay crisp for over a month in the garden, but most become hollow if not used when they are about an inch across. The Spanish and Chinese radishes used in cooking are planted in midsummer for fall and winter use. They are large and long and can be stored for months in plastic bags in a cool place.

When the Burpee White Radish was first tested at Fordhook, I learned that radish leaves are cooked and eaten in China (whence the seeds came). I cooked them and found them to be delicious. The leaves of this variety are not as hairy as those of red radishes (though all radish leaves are edible).

One late spring day I had a desire to eat something fresh and green, so I roamed around the yard with a basket and knife. I'm not fond of dandelion greens, and especially spending the time to wash them three or four times, so I did not collect them. We had horses and a wonderful compost pile. Around it I found nice young dock leaves, which I had read were edible. A few chard roots and beets had survived the winter and produced new leaves—and the radishes needed thinning. With this combination I had a meal with first greens which I enjoyed thoroughly.

Radishes are almost always eaten raw, either whole or sliced in salads. Chopped radishes are also good to use in dips on crackers. Winter types are used cooked in some Oriental dishes.

∘ Radish Dip

This recipe was given to me by my daughter. The radish pieces should be large enough to be crunchy.

8 ounces cream cheese, at room
  temperature
1 teaspoon milk
1 small clove garlic, finely
  chopped

1 tablespoon fresh dillweed or 1
  teaspoon dried
1 tablespoon lemon juice
½ teaspoon salt
1 cup chopped radishes

Mix together the cream cheese and milk until smooth and creamy. Combine with remaining ingredients and refrigerate for 30 minutes before serving. *Makes 1¾ cups.*

Other Ideas for Radishes

- Refrigerating radishes in water makes them crisper and removes some of their pungency.
- Make red radish roses by cutting "petals" all around the sides. Or make fans by slicing several times across the top and down through almost to the bottom. Place in ice water until they open out.
- Grate raw carrots and radishes and dress with a sweet-and-sour dressing. Or cook briefly and serve as a side dish.
- Slice radishes and onions into very thin rounds and toss with finely chopped fresh mint, olive oil, and lemon juice.
- The Japanese make a spicy condiment by grating large white radishes (daikon) with red chili peppers.

- Braise radishes or cook them with a cream sauce—the flavor resembles that of young turnips.
- Radish seed pods can be pickled to resemble capers or added to pickled green beans.

Rhubarb is a wonderful old-fashioned plant that is not used as much as it should be. It is a large perennial that is attractive enough to grow in the perennial border if you don't have room in your vegetable garden. Some people plant it at the ends of their asparagus beds.

Rhubarb needs lots of food. I fertilize mine in early spring just as the ground thaws, and again in August. This encourages the development of healthy roots. Rhubarb also needs good drainage; don't plant it where water is apt to stand.

It takes about three years for rhubarb to reach harvesting size. Seeds should be planted in early spring and plants thinned to a foot apart. The second year you can transplant roots to a permanent sunny location, spacing them at least three feet apart. Or you can buy rhubarb roots for faster results. When the clump produces about twelve big leaves, it is mature enough and you can pick from it without weakening the plant. Wait until the stems are a good foot long before pulling them, and then take only as much as you need at one time. When you pull rhubarb, make sure that you allow at least one leaf to develop on each small crown; otherwise you will weaken the roots.

I stop harvesting rhubarb around June 10, but in colder climates you can pick it a little later. You'll know when to stop because flower stems start to develop and the crown does not produce many new leaves. Cut the flower stalk out as soon as you see it, even though the tall spikes of white flowers are very attractive.

Rhubarb leaves are poisonous, so discard them. For the best color, do not peel the stalks. I never cook rhubarb in an aluminum pan because the metal spoils the flavor.

Rhubarb is one of the easiest garden products to freeze. Just wash and dry the stalks and put them whole into a long freezer bag, squeeze out the air, close, and freeze. Some people prefer to cut up rhubarb before freezing, but I find the packages bulky. When using frozen rhubarb, let the stalks thaw only partly before cutting because they are hard to cut into nice pieces when thawed. Use a stainless serrated knife when cutting rhubarb, as it cuts the fibers better.

∘ Stewed Rhubarb

Cut 10 rhubarb stalks (about 1¼ pounds) into ¾-inch-long pieces. Pour boiling water over them and let stand for 5 minutes. Drain and put in a glass or ceramic baking dish that can be covered. Do not fill to the top. Shake 1 cup sugar over the rhubarb and bake in a 300° oven. After 15 minutes, stir gently so all pieces are in the juice. Cover and return to the oven for 15 minutes more. Remove rhubarb from oven, taste, and add more sugar if needed. Baked rhubarb has better color than that cooked slowly on top of the stove, and the pieces retain their shape.   **Makes about 4 cups.**

Additions to stewed rhubarb: Raisins—use golden ones if you have them. Strawberries—even a few added to rhubarb are nice. A good proportion is 1 cup berries to 4 cups rhubarb. Add them after the first 15 minutes of cooking. Strawberry syrup can be used for some of the sweetening, or even strawberry jam.

Other Ideas for Rhubarb

∘ Stewed rhubarb is a refreshing sauce to serve on top of cheesecake or vanilla pudding.

○ A quick dessert is hot stewed rhubarb served on hot buttered cinnamon toast.
○ Substitute rhubarb for apples in Brown Betty. I often use rhubarb in recipes that call for some apple, adding a few raisins for richer flavor.
○ Fold sweetened cooked diced rhubarb into yogurt.
○ See recipes for Rhubarb Marmalade, Rhubarb Cake, and Rhubarb-Pineapple Sauce.

The early turnips are the purple-skinned white varieties. They are more delicate in flavor than the so-called yellow turnip, or rutabaga (discussed later), served in the fall and winter. White turnips can be ready to eat forty-five days after planting—that is, the roots. Turnip greens will be ready sooner. You can sow the seeds quite close in the furrow and thin out the row as you pick them.

If you are fond of turnip greens, you might try a variety developed for its greens, such as Burpee Foliage or Shogoin Turnip, whose tops are ready in thirty days. I find turnip greens to be a bit stringy, and I advise cutting off the leaf stems below the green of the leaves. They are a favorite vegetable of many southerners, who usually season them by boiling with bacon. I like turnip greens only when they are very young, when they can also be used raw in a mixed salad. They are very high in vitamins C and A.

My family prefer crunchy raw turnip roots to cooked ones.

When preparing raw turnips ahead of time, refrigerate them in lightly salted water.

Small fresh garden turnips bear little resemblance to the big, aging, often pithy globes you find in grocery stores. At their best, turnips resemble crisp apples or radishes in flavor. Harvest them when they are only two or three inches across, peel them (the skins are bitter), and cook in boiling water just until tender. Or steam them—whole small turnips take twenty to thirty minutes to steam tender.

Other Ideas for Turnips

- Thinly slice turnips and serve like chips with dip. Or use them in a dip (substitute them for radishes in Radish Dip; see recipe).
- Chrysanthemum turnips make a lovely appetizer or garnish. Peel small turnips, cut tops level, then cross-score the flesh as deep and finely as possible without cutting through bottoms. Soak in salt water for 20 minutes, drain, sprinkle with sweetened vinegar, and refrigerate at least one day. Using chopsticks, gently open out the "flower petals." Place a piece of red pepper or a carrot slice in the center of each "chrysanthemum."
- Stir-fry shredded turnips with scallions and other vegetables or thinly sliced ham.
- Grate turnips, carrots, and onion and toss with vinaigrette.
- Cook small turnips and their greens separately until tender, then serve them together with crumbled bacon on top.
- Mash cooked turnips as you would potatoes—or mash them with potatoes.
- Make scalloped turnips: layer thin slices with sliced onions, dotting each layer with butter and sprinkling with flour and salt. Pour in a cup or so of beef broth and bake 1½ hours at 350° F.
- For quick turnip pickles, cut turnips in fine julienne strips and finely chop the greens. Sprinkle generously with salt and knead to draw liquid out. Discard liquid and add leftover pickle juice (or your own mixture) to the turnips.

Before the days of refrigerated shipping, fresh greens were not available through the winter months, so they were a special delight to the homemaker in early spring. People used to drive to a country road and walk along the edge, carrying a knife and a bag into which they put any edible plant they could find—poke, dandelion, dock, mallow, mustard, field cress, asparagus. Some people still get a kick out of foraging today, but greens from the garden are usually handier and cleaner.

In the winter in Florida, I have seen dandelions being grown to be shipped for cooking greens (they are somewhat milder than the ones growing wild). Mustard greens are also popular in the South in winter, but we can grow them in the early garden up North, too. I like them best when only two inches tall and use them raw for a mustardy flavor in salads or in a cold meat sandwich in place of lettuce. Other greens that can go into a pot of mixed greens—collards, kale, chard, beet greens—are discussed elsewhere.

All the greens used for salads can be boiled, but it takes an awful lot of them to make several servings, since they reduce greatly in cooking. When I do not have enough of one kind, I mix them up in the pot. Strong-flavored greens like mustard and turnip are mellowed by celtuce or large outer leaves of loosehead lettuce. I also like the mixture of white radish and spinach leaves. Cook greens only until tender, not a soggy mass. Flavor the cooking liquid with bacon or a ham hock if you like, and sprinkle with vinegar or soy sauce.

Mixed greens, hot cornbread or pita bread, and cheese make a delicious lunch.

6

Summer Vegetables

The vegetables in this section need warmth for germination as well as for growth and ripening. Some of them are started indoors six to eight weeks before the last expected frost in your area. In the case of eggplant and tomato, the "days" given in catalogs mean the length of time it will take to have edible produce after you have set young plants in the garden.

It is interesting that many of the most common and popular summer vegetables in American gardens—beans, corn, tomatoes, peppers, squash, and even potatoes—were all growing in Central and South America in the sixteenth and seventeenth centuries when explorers came across the Atlantic and took seeds or tubers back to Europe. When puzzled by the behavior of seeds and plants, I have found it illuminating to look into their native habitat and get some idea of what the weather is like there.

Why do the corn seeds I plant sprout without a rain or watering, but not beans? Because corn originated where there was not much rain, but beans grew in the lowlands of Central and South America, where there is naturally more moisture. Spinach came from Arab countries, where rain falls only during the short days of the year when the weather is cool. As the days get longer, it bolts and goes to seed. That is why, even when the summer is fairly cool, succession plantings of spinach cannot be made throughout the summer; it is the longer days that make it bolt. However, it can be planted again in the fall in the South as the days get shorter.

Vegetables native to hot climates like tomato and okra will make good vegetative growth in cool weather, but they will flower and set fruit only when the weather is warm and not too wet.

Mulches

A green mulch of lawn clippings really kills weeds as it heats up in the process of decaying. For this reason it should not be placed up against the plants. A thick layer of damp, hot grass clippings will produce an unpleasant odor—let each thin layer dry out a bit before adding more.

Dry leaves are best when taken from a pile that is a year old, when they have begun to decay. A thick layer of freshly fallen leaves can become a suffocating mass above a plant's crown. Extra nitrogen should be applied on a mulch of leaves to hasten their decay by nitrogen-consuming bacteria.

Wood chips are a long-lasting mulch. They should be put on after a good rain. The chips absorb water and can keep rain from getting to the soil, but they do suppress weeds and help to keep soil moist once water is in it.

Black plastic is frequently used when growing melons, cucumbers, and sometimes tomatoes. Its use eliminates weeding and sometimes speeds ripening. Holes are made in the plastic where plants are to grow. After heavy rains pools of water form on it where there are depressions. These can become stagnant, so I poke holes in the plastic to let the water through to the soil. Black plastic makes gardening easier, but it's a mess to clean up in the fall.

I've tried using a thick layer of newspapers between rows of strawberries. It works well but is unsightly. Like all mulches it should be put down after a rain. I use it around seedling trees when I set them out, as the paper not only keeps the weeds down but also marks the location of the tree.

Do not use ordinary hay or straw, for they will introduce a multitude of weed seeds to the garden. Salt hay, which grows on the edge of ocean marshes, is comparatively weed-free. It's expensive, but it is my first choice for my strawberry bed.

Seaweed can be used on very sandy soil, where the salt in it will wash out of the soil quickly.

Almost all the beans listed in catalogs are native American plants except fava beans and soybeans. Some beans were grown by the Indians as far north as Canada, and these no doubt were of the quicker-flowering string-bean type, which produce small dried beans and have tough pods. The old string beans are now called snap beans because through breeding, the strings have been eliminated. Early beans were all pole beans, and it was also through breeding and selection that dwarf varieties became available.

Most beans are very sensitive to cold so should not be planted until all danger of frost has gone. They need quite a bit of moisture in the soil to germinate. Germination can be hastened a bit by soaking the seeds for not more than eight hours before planting. It is safer to soak them for a short time than long—the seeds split when soaked too long.

There are really no special tricks to growing beans. Make sure the plants are not crowded in the row—thin them by snipping off unwanted seedlings so remaining plants stand two to four inches apart. I pull the soil up around the base of the plants as they develop. This gives them a firmer hold in the ground so they don't topple over when they bear.

Each season I make several plantings of green bush beans. When I see the flower buds on the first planting I know it's time to sow the next row. I've planted beans as late as August 15 and had a fair crop in early October. When frost was threatening I protected the plants with plastic cloches. This last picking has always seemed especially good because it was a chance I took late in the season.

When I pick beans I always use two hands—one hand on the pod and one below its stem. Bean pods grow in clusters that usually contain both mature and young ones. If the mature bean is yanked off, the whole cluster often breaks off too, and part of the crop is lost.

Bean plants must be watched carefully for the juicy little yellow bean beetle grub. As soon as I see the first one, I get out the rotenone (or Sevin). I always pick my beans before I apply the rotenone. This means early-morning picking because the powder won't stick unless the leaves are slightly damp. It's important to get the rotenone on the underside of the leaves where the bean beetles are.

Bush snap beans, which grow fifteen to twenty inches tall, can be picked in about fifty days from seed planting. One sowing will produce nicely for only three to four weeks, so it is best to make several plantings. Pole beans, which need a sturdy support, take about ten days longer to bear, but they will continue to produce unless there is a hot, dry spell. It seems to me that pole beans do better when the weather is cooler than it is here in Pennsylvania. I was amazed at how good their flavor was in Lompoc, California, where owing to cool ocean breezes the temperature seldom rises above 75° F. To counteract the heat here in Pennsylvania, I have been growing my pole beans— such as Romano and Burpee Golden—where they are shaded after two in the afternoon, and the vines have been healthier.

It's nice to grow a variety of beans. There is quite a difference in flavor and texture from one variety to another, and beans can be served several times in one week without becoming monotonous. Burpee's Tenderpod and Brittle Wax bush beans and Burpee Golden and Romano pole beans give you four different flavors.

I find round-podded beans excellent for snapping or cutting and many of the flatter varieties more suitable for frenching. Any of the snap beans, when older, can be made tastier and more tender by frenching.

Green and Yellow Snap Beans

The distinctive flavor of snap beans is tasted only when they are cooked beyond the *al dente* stage and the raw flavor has gone, but when cooked too long they lose most of their flavor. I always have a kettle of boiling water on the stove when I am cooking vegetables, for I put the vegetables in a pot, pour boiling water over to cover them, and keep the heat on high so the water will return to boiling quickly. This way all the beans, or whatever, will cook evenly, which is not the case with steam cooking. After the water has returned to a boil, leave the lid off so you can test the beans frequently and know just when they are done. This is where my granny fork comes in handy.

It takes about twenty minutes for four cups of cut beans to cook. When done, drain the water off immediately, set the pot on a low burner, and stir the beans around a bit to get rid of any water inside the pods. Then add butter and seasoning and serve in a warm dish.

For variety I sometimes mix yellow and green beans or add a sprig or two of summer savory to the water when cooking green beans. The color of yellow or wax beans is a bit dull, so I brighten them by adding some chopped fresh parsley when ready to serve.

Romano and Burpee Golden Beans

Because the pods of these pole beans are flattish and nearly an inch wide and their texture different from ordinary snap beans, they are almost like a different vegetable. They are slightly mealy, so they absorb water and cook faster than ordinary snap beans. A string will develop on the straight side as these beans get older. This should be removed.

I tried frenching Romano beans once and they were awful—all the flavor went and they had no character. But you can vary the way you cut them across, either straight or at an angle. Two cups of Romano beans will cook in boiling water in eight to ten minutes. For a novelty I have served Romano beans with hot bacon dressing: Blanch the beans until just warm through and drain thoroughly. Then cook like Celtuce Leaves with Bacon Dressing. The beans should still be firm, not mushy, when served.

Burpee golden beans have a very delicate flavor. The beans inside the pod are green and the pods have a brighter yellow color when the vines are not crowded. Cut the beans in one-inch lengths and cook in only a little water until just tender, about eight minutes. Do not cover. Pour water off and put back on low heat to dry off a bit. Add a generous amount of butter to the beans. Add chopped parsley just before serving.

For a pole bean that is both beautiful and edible, grow Scarlet Runner. The flowers are brilliant, the pods are long with a rough surface and are eaten like snapbeans, and mature beans can be shelled out. They produce better in cooler areas. I remember seeing them growing two stories high in the winter in Palestine.

Lima Beans

Lima beans are a relatively slow-to-bear plant and can be disappointing to the gardener anxious for a quick crop. Bush limas are ready to harvest much sooner than pole limas, but the crop will come and go quickly. Pole limas will keep on bearing until frost and, in my opinion, have better texture and flavor than bush limas.

A distinction is often made between fat, large-seeded, mealy "potato" limas (such as Burpee's Fordhook) and the smaller, flatter baby butter beans (such as Henderson Bush limas). Any lima beans can be dried, and they freeze well.

Limas are at their best when young, with bright green pods. The pods do not split open easily at this stage, so I use my swivel peeler and rip it down the straight edge where the beans are fastened to the pod. Do all the ripping first, then shell. To cook, pour boiling water over the beans. Use a large pot because limas make the water foam up and boil over readily. Taste frequently, as time for cooking depends on age and size of bean.

Should your beans get old, put one-quarter teaspoon baking soda on them, add boiling water, and cook for three minutes. Then pour water off, add fresh hot water, and cook ten minutes more. This method softens the outer coat of the beans, so they are more digestible, and retains their color. It does not destroy the vitamin content of the beans as much as having soda in the water the entire time the beans are cooking.

As lima beans are usually a little mealy, they should be served moist; do not skimp on the butter. I like to serve limas as a side dish when serving a stew without potatoes in it.

Shell Beans

The seeds of all the beans can be dried and eaten, but some are grown only for *dry* shell beans. The most common are Red Kidney, White Marrowfat, and Pinto beans. These beans must mature on the plants; their seeds should be sown as soon as all danger of frost is over so that the plants will have three warm months in which to grow.

I do not harvest and store dried shell beans generally as my family does not care for them. But I like baked beans once in a while, and this is how I prepare them.

○ Baked Beans

2 cups dried beans	2 tablespoons ketchup
2 medium onions	1 tablespoon vinegar
4 slices bacon, chopped	¼ teaspoon salt
2 tablespoons molasses	

Soak the dried beans overnight in cold water. Drain and cook in fresh water. Watch the pot, for the water may foam up and boil over. Drain as soon as they have come to a boil, then cook longer in fresh hot water until the skins on the beans split when you blow on them. This water will not foam up so much. Drain the beans, saving 2 cups of the water.

Put the beans into a crock that has a lid, layering with the onions and bacon. Mix the other ingredients with the 2 cups of reserved water and pour over the beans. Bake covered at 325° F. for at least 2 hours or cook in an electric crock pot.   *Serves 6.*

Soybeans

Soybeans, natives of Asia, are being grown more by home gardeners in recent years because of their high protein content. I grew them only once to use when green and gave up, as they took a lot of space and were hard to shell. Pouring hot water over the green pods or boiling them for ten minutes makes them easier to open, but it still took too much time to suit me and I didn't care for their flavor or very firm texture. To grow them, you need a long summer—they take up to 120 days to mature, though you may harvest them earlier and cook them like lima beans. To dry soybeans, let the pods turn brown on the stalks. I do enjoy soybean sprouts, which I grow in a large glass jar through the winter and early spring.

Fava Beans

The fava bean (or broad bean), a pod bean like limas, is native to Europe. Favas are fascinating-looking upright plants that must be grown in cool weather. They grow well in New England if started indoors.

Although fava beans are delicately flavored and tender when they are no larger than a thumbnail (and, when smaller than that, may be eaten pods and all), their skin gets increasingly tough and bitter as the beans get bigger. To serve mature fava beans, you should slip off the skins after cooking them.

Other Beans

Black-eyed peas are a bean, but they are members of a different genus from common garden beans. They are a native African bean.

Mung beans, which are used mostly for sprouting, are native to southern Asia.

So beans are not just beans. You can do a great deal of exploring with them. The shapes and colors of bean seeds are fascinating, and this is how many of the types and varieties are identified. They range in color from white through brown to black. The scarlet runners are black with bright red—many are speckled.

Other Ideas for Beans

- Savory is known as the "bean herb." Put a sprig in the pot for variety in flavor when cooking beans.
- Snap beans are delicious stir-fried or cooked whole in batter as tempura.

- Instead of making the predictable three-bean salad, use any green or yellow beans and beans from pod beans that have grown too old but not yet dry. Add lots of chives and an oil-and-vinegar dressing.
- Make a salad with different-colored shell beans and add some diced celery to lighten its texture. Use a mustardy vinaigrette dressing.
- See recipes for Golden Beet and Green Bean Salad; Fordhook Succotash.
- Try a sweet-and-sour sauce or a marinara sauce with snap beans or limas.
- Purée green beans and whip them with potatoes.
- Whole young snap beans make delicious dill-garlic pickles.
- If beans are a bit over the hill, cook them the southern way— long and slowly with a ham hock.
- Save any leftover beans; marinate them in an oil dressing just before adding to salads.
- A few green beans added to chicken or fish casseroles made with a cream sauce make the dish more attractive, and they certainly can improve the looks of canned soups.

Most beet seeds are actually little hard clusters of several seeds. I get best germination if I soak the seeds overnight before planting. I sow both the early and the late varieties so I can get all my planting done at the same time. For small gardens I highly recommend Cylindra, a variety with a long root that stays sweet even when old. Lutz Green Leaf beet is a slow-growing large beet not very attractive to look at, but it has a delicious sweet flavor and is a very good keeper. The roots live over winter in the garden and produce young green leaves in the spring. It is called Green Leaf because the leaves do not have red veins.

Beets are not difficult to grow, but they do have a way of pushing themselves out of the ground. I pull the soil up around the plants several times during the season so the top of the root is always covered. This is especially important with Burpee's Golden Beet; it will lose its delicate flavor and color if exposed to the sun.

The only real problem with growing beets is that the leaves are a favorite food of rabbits and slugs. A few slugs can eat a whole row of beet seedlings overnight. I learned this from sad experience: one afternoon I saw a nice row of beet seedlings; when I came down to the garden the next morning there wasn't a single plant.

The flavor of beets varies greatly according to the mineral content of the soil (beets do not like acid soil) and the speed with which the beets develop (they prefer cooler weather). The best-flavored beets I have ever tasted were grown in a garden mulched with seaweed.

There is more than just a difference in color between the golden beet and the red beet. The flavor of golden beets is more delicate

Discouraging the Slugs

To combat slugs I use diatomaceous earth, a substance made up of tiny, sharp-pointed granules. Slugs will not crawl over it. When I plant my beets I scatter diatomaceous earth over the rows. Check the garden after a heavy rain; you may have to reapply it. You can also use diatomaceous earth in the asparagus and strawberry patches—other favorite spots for slugs. This useful garden aid is most easily available from swimming-pool supply stores, which sell it in large quantities as a water filter for pools. Never handle diatomaceous earth with bare hands.

and sweeter, and the beet does not discolor whatever it comes in contact with. It also retains its flavor and tenderness throughout the growing season. This is true of its foliage as well, which is more succulent and has a heavier texture than red beets. Do not hesitate to serve the greens and the roots of golden beets at the same meal as separate vegetables—their flavors are quite different.

○ Beet Greens

When I thin the rows of beets I use the tender young plants for greens. The foliage of golden beets is exceptionally good at any age, and because there is no red in the veins, it stays bright and green when cooked in an open pot. Beet greens have a lovely, delicate flavor, not as strong as spinach. I prepare the greens the same way I cook spinach. Some people add bacon for flavor, but I just use butter. I don't like to hide the flavor of vegetables.

○ Beets with Orange Sauce

This recipe is from Alex Hawkes's *The World of Vegetable Cookery.*

3 tablespoons coarsely grated
  orange rind
1 cup orange juice
½ teaspoon salt
1 tablespoon cornstarch

⅓ cup butter
Pepper to taste
4 cups diced, sliced, or shredded
  cooked beets

Cook all but the beets in a double boiler until smooth and clear. Add beets and heat through.   *Serves 8.*

°Cold Red Beets

When preparing beets for a salad, I add the salt while the slices are still warm—they seem to absorb it better then. Do not cover hot sliced beets, because they will lose their firm texture and deep red color.

I serve marinated sliced red beets as a side dish with cold beef. With them I like a touch of bay leaf or sweet basil, which I add to the warm sliced beets along with an oil-and-vinegar dressing. Stir occasionally for about 5 minutes over low heat. Then cool and add onion slices. Remove the bay leaf or basil before serving.

°Molded Red Beet Salad

This is a nice salad to have at a buffet, with lots of crisp lettuce or escarole on the platter around it, when you are serving cold meats. It gives the appearance of being a cranberry salad, and it is good with turkey. I advise preparing this a day ahead of time. Serve it with a dressing of half mayonnaise and half sour cream.

2 quarts whole fresh beets
3 bay leaves or 2 sprigs fresh basil
Four 3-ounce packages lemon-
   flavored gelatin
1½ teaspoons salt

¾ cup white vinegar
¼ cup grated fresh horseradish
   (preferred) or ⅓ cup
   commercially bottled
⅓ cup grated onion
2 cups finely diced celery, strings
   removed

Scrub the beets clean and cook in not less than 2 quarts water. Add the bay leaves or basil to the water and cook until a fork pierces the beets easily. Drain and save the water. Remove the bay leaves or basil. Let the beets cool, then peel and dice them. You should have about 4 cups.

Bring to a boil 3 cups of the beet cooking water and dissolve gelatin in it. Add 4 cups cool beet water, salt, and vinegar. Let this cool until it thickens to the consistency of raw egg white. Add the beets, horseradish, onion, and celery. Mix well and pour into a lightly oiled pan or a shallow bowl that will hold 3½ quarts. Chill.

Serves 12.

∘ Golden Beet Pickle

When golden beets were first introduced, I had to think of some unusual way to serve them to a large group of garden writers at a buffet luncheon. I thought that as a pickle they could be featured as a cocktail snack. Since the sweeter flavor of golden beets is one of their attributes, I decided to make a sweet pickle. Although red beets are often made into a sour pickle, you can use this same recipe with red beets too.

Any leftover pickle brine is good for basting ham, pork, or lamb, or for making cucumber bread-and-butter pickles, or for marinating leftover vegetables.

24 beets, about 2 inches in
  diameter
6-7 onions, about 2 inches in
  diameter, sliced
5 cups white vinegar
5 cups sugar
3 teaspoons salt

1½ teaspoons turmeric
1 tablespoon marigold petals
  (optional)
2 teaspoons mustard seed
1 teaspoon celery seed

Wash the beets and boil in a large pot of water until almost tender, 30 minutes at most. Drain, peel and slice the beets. Return the beets to the pot, making alternate layers of beets and onion slices. In a saucepan, prepare pickle brine with remaining ingredients. Heat brine until sugar melts. Add to beets and onions and heat very slowly to a low boil. Spoon into sterilized jars and seal at once.

Makes about 5 pints.

∘ Golden Beet and Green Bean Salad

2 cups green snap beans, cut into
  1-inch lengths
2 cups diced cooked golden beets
1 cup thinly sliced celery, strings
  removed
¼ cup chopped Bermuda onion
¼ cup peeled green pepper cut in
  small pieces

Young celery leaves from heart of
  celery, cut up
½ cup Old-Fashioned French
  Dressing (page 43)
¼ cup chopped parsley or dill
Lettuce

Cook snap beans just until raw taste has gone. Combine with remaining ingredients (except lettuce), toss, and chill. Serve on a bed of lettuce. *Serves 6.*

Other Ideas for Beets

- Many herbs go well with beets—try basil, dill, rosemary, horseradish, chives.
- Shred raw beets and toss with vinaigrette and lots of chopped parsley. Shredded celeriac goes well with it. Or use a dressing made with yogurt.
- For a very special dish, I use an orange glaze on golden beets.
- For an unusual appetizer, hollow out small cooked beets, marinate in vinaigrette, then stuff with egg salad.
- Try Harvard beets in a citrus sauce, using lemon juice and grated rind instead of vinegar.
- Borscht is a good way to use old beets; I combine shredded beets, tomatoes, celery, carrots, red cabbage and broth and cook this mixture for an hour. See also recipe for Borscht Concentrate for the Freezer.
- Pickle peeled hard-boiled eggs in red beet pickle juice.
- A refreshing approach to salad: Tear the leaves of a young fresh lettuce, such as romaine, cut up a celery-heart stalk with its leaves, and combine with some Golden Beet Pickle, dressing it lightly with some of the pickle brine and a little oil.
- To make red-flannel hash, combine finely chopped beets, potatoes, corned beef, and onions. Moisten with milk and fry in fat until brown and crusty.
- See recipe for Golden Beet Dip.

Garden-fresh broccoli is so much more delicate in flavor and texture than what I find in the stores that I never buy any. People talk about fresh corn and fresh asparagus, but I think the difference in fresh broccoli is even greater. I have noticed that broccoli heads even one day old take longer to cook than just-picked ones. Broccoli can have a sweet, refreshing flavor or a heavy, dominating one, depending on the temperature during its heading and the speed with which it gets into the pot.

Broccoli seed should be started indoors. I set the young plants out as soon as the garden soil is ready after the last hard frost. I always set my broccoli plants quite deep, covering the first two sets of leaves but not the growing tips. Broccoli has shallow roots, so if the plants are not set firmly in the ground they will topple over as the heads develop. Plants should be spaced at least a foot apart.

Because I am naturally lazy, I prefer the sprouting type of broccoli—De Cicco (Burpee's Greenbud Brand) or Green Goliath—rather than the single-head varieties (such as Premium Crop Hybrid), for spring planting, because one planting is all I will need for broccoli all summer long. The central heads (which are really flower buds) appear suddenly. If they are picked frequently, the plants will produce smaller side-branch heads for at least two months. I cut the stalk of the first head above any leaves to leave plenty of stalk from which the later crop heads can develop.

I am particularly fond of a late fall crop of broccoli because cool weather sweetens the taste. In early August I set out plants of a single-head (nonsprouting) variety, which produces large heads all at once, timed to ensure a cool-weather harvest, which has the best flavor.

Broccoli requires plenty of fertilizer to give it a vigorous start and produce large heads. I use a starter solution when setting out the plants, and then about four weeks later I apply a side dressing of 5-10-10 fertilizer.

Flea beetles find young broccoli plants very tempting, so I dust with rotenone; the beetles are not a problem for late plantings. I watch for cabbage worms, which can also be banished by rotenone.

As with the squash family, there is invariably too much broccoli ready at one time. Fortunately, it freezes very well. The fall crop produces large heads that are tighter and better for freezing than the sprouting type. To freeze broccoli, be sure to pick the heads before they loosen up.

I cut broccoli heads so that the pieces are about 3 inches long, arrange them in a steamer rack with flower heads up, put it in a pot that is deeper than the rack, shake ½ teaspoon of salt over the broccoli, then pour boiling water over the heads until I see water halfway up the stems. Cover the pot with a spatter cover, not a solid lid, and boil rapidly for about 8 minutes. Always test for doneness by pricking stem with a fork or by tasting cooking time depends on the age and quantity of broccoli. It should be well drained before serving. I like to season with only butter or bread crumbs lightly browned in hot butter or margarine—1 teaspoon crumbs to 1 tablespoon butter. Or a little Parmesan cheese is nice.

The stems of broccoli heads can be peeled and sliced raw to use in a salad, or boiled until tender and served with a cream or cheese sauce. They do not have quite the flavor of the flower heads, but the texture is pleasant when broccoli stems are cooked just crunch-tender.

Later in the summer, the side heads that sprout are smaller: an Indian woman taught me a delicious way to use these:

○ *Broccoli in Ginger-Flavored Oil*

Put about ¼ cup of chickpea flour or whole-wheat flour in a paper bag. Shake some salt into it. Wash broccoli sprouts, shake them almost dry, then shake them in the bag with flour. Heat a thin layer of oil in a frying pan with 4–5 slices of fresh ginger root. Soak ginger in the oil over low heat for 15 minutes, then remove. Raise the heat to medium high. Remove broccoli from the bag, place in pan, and stir-fry. I was always surprised at how long this woman cooked it—45 minutes. All the ginger-flavored oil is absorbed by the broccoli. (The Indians have a theory that ginger makes all the cabbage-family vegetables more digestible.)

Other Ideas for Broccoli

- Chervil, dill, and oregano go well with broccoli, as do caraway seeds, a little nutmeg, and curry powder.
- If you suspect there are insects in your broccoli head, soak it for 30 minutes in salty water—this also crisps it.
- Use bits of broccoli to add color to egg dishes: quiches, soufflés, frittate, omelets.
- Julienne broccoli stems and carrots and stir-fry or steam them together for a nice color combination.
- Purée broccoli and use instead of avocados in making guacamole.
- For a stunning presentation, cook broccoli and cauliflower until barely tender and pack flowerets, stems up, around the inside of a bowl. Fill the center with leftover bits, place a plate on top, and invert for a rounded broccoli-cauliflower "head." Serve cold with curried mayonnaise or hot with lemon butter or hollandaise.
- Place cooked broccoli flowerets decoratively on a casserole of creamed fish, chicken, or turkey.
- Leftover broccoli can be marinated in an oil-and-vinegar dressing—good served on the side of a plate with a hot grilled-cheese sandwich.

Cabbage is usually thought of as a fall vegetable (see later discussion), but there are some early varieties, such as Earliana, that head quickly and, when seed is sown indoors, will do well in the early summer garden. Because of their quick growth, I think their flavor is more delicate than that of fall and winter cabbage. The heads are smaller and the midribs not as thick. The days mentioned in catalogs describing the varieties are the length of time it takes for a head to mature from setting out the young plants—about 65 days.

Early cabbage heads will not stay in good shape in the garden. They are apt to split after a heavy rain and rot as soon as the days are hot—keep this in mind as you harvest your crop. Put the heads in ventilated plastic bags and keep in a cool place or refrigerator.

I like early cabbage cooked very lightly, so it is still a bit crispy, with butter and parsley added. It is also better stir-fried than winter cabbage.

○ *Stir-Fried Cabbage*

Place a thin layer of vegetable oil in a heavy pan and add 4 or 5 slices of fresh ginger root while the oil is heating (do not let it smoke). Cook the ginger in the oil for 15 minutes, then remove and add shredded cabbage. Cover with a spatter lid and stir occasionally until it is cooked to your taste. Season with salt and about ½ teaspoon cumin seed for each 4 cups raw cabbage.

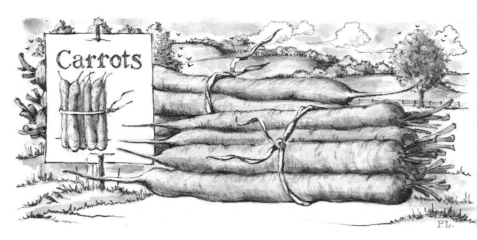

Ever since it became popular to serve carrots raw to nibble as sticks or enjoy in a salad, this vegetable has risen in popularity. In my opinion, carrots should always be kept on hand in the refrigerator or in the garden. To be without a carrot is almost as bad as running out of sugar—some carrot or carrot juice improves the flavor of numerous dishes.

The one snack I let my children have without asking was raw carrots. They were allowed to pull them from the cold frame in which I grew them at that time. Recently, my daughter was recalling, with laughter, her childhood raids on the carrot patch, hopefully unobserved by anyone, as they played their games of "goodies and baddies," copying the children's radio stories of those days.

In my first garden the carrots were tasteless and malformed because the soil was so heavy. It is only after improving the soil with a lot of mulch that I can now grow a sweet carrot. Those in the markets are grown in muck land, and that is how they get so long. In the home garden, work the soil deeply and rake out clods and stones. Seedsmen have developed carrots for all types of soil, and I advise new gardeners to select short and thicker varieties, such as Short 'n Sweet, Goldinhart, and Chantenay.

All root vegetables must be planted where they are to grow as soon as the soil has warmed up and will crumble. Carrot seeds are small and stick together, so it is almost impossible to sow the seeds thin enough for the roots to develop well without thinning. (Don't count on rabbits to do it, for, contrary to the story of Peter Rabbit, carrots are not rabbits' favorite seedling. Beets are.) Since carrots are slow to germinate, it is a good idea to mix a few radish seeds in with them and sow them at the same time. The radishes will mark the row and as you pull them will give space for the carrots to develop. If carrots are crowded, they become misshapen. The roots should also be kept well covered with soil to prevent green shoulders.

If you can grow tasty carrots, make two plantings a month or more apart; old carrots get woody, lose flavor, and split lengthwise in the soil. The sweetest and tenderest part of carrots is the brighter outside part—discard the tough cores of older carrots.

Imagination in the use of carrots can lift them from a humble status, which they do not deserve. They are very good food as well as being a colorful spot on a plate. They are more flavorful when not peeled—nonmetal pot scrubbers are great for cleaning them—though using a peeler is sometimes necessary. Carrots can be cut across diagonally, in strips, and in crinkled pieces with a special cutter. They can also be coarsely or finely grated. Young carrots are best left whole. The cooking time depends on the size of the pieces—just be careful not to overcook. Boil carrots in enough salted water to cover them, keeping pot covered, and taste frequently for doneness. Grated carrots naturally take less time; be sure to save the cooking water for soups. Drain the carrots and return them to the pot for seasoning. Put pot on low heat and get rid of all the water. This brings out the flavor. Add the amount of butter you like—one tablespoon for two cups cooked carrots is plenty—and some sugar or marmalade if you want to glaze them.

○ *Carrots with Celery*

Carrots with celery is my favorite vegetable dish to serve with fish. Cut carrots across. String celery and cut outside green stalks into pieces of the same size. Cook carrots in lightly salted water for 10 minutes before adding the celery. Boil covered for 10 minutes more. When done, drain and add butter and finely chopped celery leaves.

○ Carrot Juice

Fresh carrot juice is just wonderful! It should be made in a juicer just before serving—otherwise the color gets dull and some sweetness goes. (People have thought I added coconut to my fresh juice.) Of course, carrot juice is good mixed with tomato juice and served cold as a beverage or heated as a soup. Serve with a sprinkle of parsley or chives mixed in sour cream. See Carrot and Tomato Broth.

Other Ideas for Carrots

- ○ Bring out the color of carrots by adding chopped parsley or chervil for contrast and eye appeal. Grated carrots can be dressed up with all kinds of seasoning: if serving with fish, use chopped chives; with poultry, add a teaspoon or two of honey, or a little nutmeg, mace, or orange rind.
- ○ Shred carrots and turnips and dress with chopped mint and vinaigrette for salad, or steam for a side dish.
- ○ Carrots are essential in a mirepoix with celery and onions to make an aromatic bed under roasting meat.
- ○ Carrots are so sweet that they can be used like fruit: add grated carrots to cakes, cookies, and pies. See recipe for Carrot Drop Cookies.
- ○ Bake small whole carrots, small potatoes, and whole onions with plenty of melted butter at 350° F. for an hour.
- ○ Cook diced carrots and potatoes in chicken stock, add cream, and purée for carrot vichyssoise.
- ○ For carrot curry, simmer carrot slices in orange juice with raisins, sliced banana, and curry powder. Thicken with cornstarch and serve on rice.
- ○ Make carrot marmalade with shredded carrots and lemon and orange rind.
- ○ See Purée of Carrot Soup.

I do not know of any vegetable that is greeted with more glee when it first arrives on the table than fresh corn on the cob. Corn is the most conspicuous plant growing in a garden, and the whole family becomes impatient for the first sweet ears.

Unfortunately, the birds and raccoons are just as eager to raid the patch. (I also had one dog who found sweet corn irresistible.) The most effective way I have found to keep wildlife away is to have a radio playing in the garden. We cut the bottom from a gallon plastic bottle, put the radio inside so it was protected from rain, hung it on a stake placed in the corn patch, then tuned in to a pop music station. I did not test to see if my patch produced better with music (as some corn growers claim), but I do know it used up a lot of batteries.

Sweet corn was originally white. The first sweet yellow corn, Golden Bantam, was introduced to gardeners by W. Atlee Burpee in 1902. Although it matured earlier, it was not popular at first—it took time to convince gardeners a yellow corn could be sweet, since they associated yellow corn with field varieties used as fodder. Breeders then worked with yellow corns and got them to produce ears as quickly as seventy-two days. More recently they have developed white corn varieties, such as White Sunglow and Silver Sweet, which can be picked in sixty-five days with good growing conditions.

Early corn varieties have smaller ears and in my experience are less problem-free than later ones. The stronger the plants the better the crop, so I plant three or four short rows of an early corn and make a larger planting of a later variety at the same time. Then three weeks later I make another planting of the same later variety. Be sure to check the days to maturity when you plant so that the corn will be best when you are home and not on vacation. The corn will not stay sweet on the stalk for your return.

When planting corn, either have plenty of defenses ready against crows or use a surplus of seed. My defenses are a tarlike Crow Repellent or Hotkaps. I mix the seeds in a paper cup with just enough repellent to coat them. After planting I mix some soil and repellent and shake that on top of the row. Sow the seed twice as thick as the plants should grow, then thin plants to eight to twelve inches apart.

Another way to foil the birds is to plant the seeds in hills about a foot in diameter. Sow the seeds in a circle, at least six seeds to a hill, then cover with a Hotkap which has been slashed open at the top to allow rain in. This may seem like a lot of work, but it is worth it to have really fresh corn from the garden. Thin hilled corn to three or four plants in each group; if four, make the hills farther apart.

Corn needs a lot of room, so it is a not a plant for a small garden. It is also a heavy feeder, requiring high-nitrogen fertilizer for best growth. It is important that plants not be so close together that their leaves cover developing ears and prevent pollen from landing on the silk. Sometimes I do some leaf pruning to expose young ears. Insects like the silk, and it is at the tip of a developing ear that eggs of the corn borer are laid. So I dust the silk frequently with rote-

Cross-Pollination in the Garden

I do not select a number of different varieties of corn, lest the ears become cross-pollinated and not produce the variety selected. Corn kernels are part of the next-generation plant (as are lima beans). Most other vegetables are part of the parent plant and are not affected by another variety's pollen. (The old wives' tale that cucumber plants will affect the flavor of melons growing nearby is not true.)

none. I have made a handy duster from a can with nail holes punched in the bottom.

The sugar in corn starts turning into starch after picking and as it gets old. Keeping picked ears cool slows down this process. As it's not always practical to go to the garden just before mealtime to gather corn, you can pick it in the cool of the morning, husk it, place the ears in a plastic bag, and refrigerate. When husking and removing the silk, always pull the husks and silk down toward the stem. Then use a clean vegetable brush and brush the remaining bits of silk down and off. If you brush up, the silk gets caught between the kernels.

It is good to have corn scorers, which can now be bought in most kitchen-supply departments. They look like small curved hoes with tines spaced to cut into the kernels of corn when drawn along the length of the cob. With the kernels cut open, you get less skin as you bite the corn off the cob.

◦ *Corn on the Cob*

Add freshly husked corn to a large pot of boiling water. Do not add salt—it toughens the skin. After the water has returned to a boil, cook for 3 more minutes. Serve wrapped in a cloth napkin. Have a scorer at each person's place to cut into the kernels before adding butter. Try eating without butter, only salt, to cut down on calories. Or, if you are on a salt-restricted diet, use unsalted butter to which you have added a few finely chopped herbs, such as dill, parsley, tarragon, or savory. I eat it without anything added and get the full flavor of the corn.

◦ *Creamed Corn*

This is a way to have corn without the hard-to-digest skin of the kernels. Put ears in boiling water, a few at a time, and remove them as soon as it has returned to a boil. Cool the ears under cold water. Take a scorer and run it up and down the ear. Hold the ear tip down on a plate and, with the back of a firm knife, scrape the insides of the kernels out, starting at the tip and working up. If you don't press too hard, the skins remain on the cob like empty honey-comb.

It is easier to scrape out raw corn, but the milk in the corn will spurt all over your kitchen. If you choose to do it raw, spread plenty of newspapers around.

Warm the scraped corn in a double boiler or, if the oven is being used anyway, in a casserole in the oven. Add butter and a little salt. Stir now and then. If your corn is a bit old, some milk and a little sugar will revive it.

I like creamed corn with chicken and turkey. It's also good with ham. Include a green vegetable in the meal.

○ Roasted Corn

Soak unhusked corn in water for about 10 minutes, then bake in a 400° oven or on the grill (turning occasionally) for 20–30 minutes, depending on size and freshness.

You can also husk corn, brush with melted butter, sprinkle with a chopped herb if you like, wrap individually in foil, and roast or grill for fifteen to twenty minutes.

○ Corn Pudding

Corn pudding is very good to serve as part of an all-vegetable meal. Feature it as the main dish. Include beets and a green vegetable.

4 cups scraped fresh corn (3-4 ears)	1 tablespoon sugar (if not using extra-sweet corn)
½ cup butter	2 tablespoons salt
	6 eggs

Mix corn, butter, sugar, and salt and heat in the top of a double boiler or in a heavy pot until corn feels hot to your finger (it's better to have it too cool than too hot). This sets the "milk" of the corn.

Beat the eggs slightly and stir into the heated corn mixture. Pour into a greased 2-quart casserole or baking dish. Set casserole in a pan of water and bake in a 350° oven until done—45–60 minutes.

If you are not ready to serve it, keep in the oven but lower temperature to 200° F.   *Serves 5-6.*

Variation: To make a fluffy-topped pudding, separate 3 of the eggs.
Beat the 3 whole eggs and 3 yolks, mix well into the corn mixture,
and place in casserole. Beat the 3 whites separately until stiff and
fold into the corn mixture. This should be served as soon as it is
done because it will fall if cooled.

○ *Fordhook Succotash*

1 cup scraped cooked corn   ½ tablespoon butter
1½ cups cooked sliced green beans

Heat the corn in the top of a double boiler, add hot beans and butter, and heat through. Do not cover.   *Serves 4.*

○ *Yellow Corn and Squash Frittata*

This is a basic recipe that can be varied by the addition of other
flavors from the garden. I prefer it made with crookneck squash or
yellow zucchini. It makes a nice luncheon dish for two or three
people. It is like a firm omelet.

2 tablespoons flour   1 summer squash (5-6 inches
¼ teaspoon salt   long), coarsely grated
¼ teaspoon baking powder   1 cup scraped corn
2 large eggs, beaten   1½ tablespoons butter, melted

Mix flour, salt, and baking powder together, then mix with eggs,
squash, corn, and 1 tablespoon melted butter. Heat ½ tablespoon
butter in a heavy 8-inch fry pan. Add mixture and cook, covered,
over medium-low heat for 15–20 minutes.

You can also bake the mixture in a buttered casserole. Cook,
uncovered, in a 325° oven for about 20 minutes, or until firm.

Serves 2-3.

Variations: Add 1 tablespoon chopped sweet peppers or 2 teaspoons chopped chives, parsley, or chervil (stronger-flavored herbs disguise the delicate flavor of the squash and corn).

Other Ideas for Corn

- ○ Add corn kernels to egg dishes: omelet, scrambled eggs, quiche, soufflé.
- ○ Dry corn: Blanch ears for 2 minutes, cut kernels off cob, spread on baking sheets, and roast at 175° F. for 12–15 hours, stirring occasionally.
- ○ Really old corn is not sweet and is very sticky when cooked. It's good only to add to pancake batter—one-third corn to two-thirds pancake mix—or to use in cream of corn soup.
- ○ Add corn to clam or fish chowder, or make chicken-corn soup, adding noodles if you like.
- ○ Use corn in stir-fry dishes, or simply stir-fry raw corn kernels with sliced scallions and green peppers.
- ○ Make corn relish, using your favorite pickling brine and adding other vegetables of your choice—cucumbers, onions, celery, peppers, cabbage.
- ○ Add leftover corn kernels to cold vegetable salads, pasta salad, or rice salad.
- ○ Leftover creamed corn makes a delicious addition to cornbread and muffins.
- ○ See Cream of Corn Soup.

Arab shepherds and muleteers have for centuries carried cucumbers instead of water to quench their thirst. Cucumbers have a long history as a cultivated vegetable and have been found growing in all parts of the world. They are not particularly nutritious but are refreshing and considered stimulating to the appetite.

Cucumbers are easy to grow if you have soil that is reasonably light, well drained but moist, and rich in organic matter—cucumbers are heavy feeders. They do best when sown directly in the garden, though they can be started indoors in individual peat pots. I sow the seeds in hills and protect each hill with a Hotkap after planting. As the seedlings emerge, I cut a crisscross in the top of each Hotkap to allow light and rain to enter. The Hotkaps also protect my plants from the birds. Young cucumber plants are their delight.

Except for the new bush types, cucumbers need space for the vines to run. Hills should be spaced four or five feet apart, with each mound thinned to two or three plants. An open mulch will conserve moisture and keep the fruit clean. Do not use lawn clippings.

The new long, slender cucumbers like Burpless Hybrid and Green Knight Hybrid produce straighter, better-looking fruits if you give them a support to climb on. They can be planted only six inches apart. I like these varieties for pickles because they make uniform slices and have a smaller diameter than other types. They are not very resistant to mosaic and mildew, however, so in addition to them I plant varieties that have good disease resistance, like Burpee's M & M Hybrid.

Unless you grow some of the disease-resistant varieties, you might wake up some morning to find all your cucumber plants wilted. In that case, it is best to pull those plants out and start over again in another section of your garden. Cut off all yellow and wilted leaves as soon as you spot them to keep disease from spreading. There are specific sprays and powders for cucumber and squash beetles, which carry wilt.

To get the best cucumber harvest, pick the fruits as soon as they are the right size. This depends on variety. Tiny gherkins should be picked when only a few inches long. Most cucumbers are best at about six inches, but some Asian varieties are fine at nearly two feet (and even oversized yellowed cucumbers that you overlooked while picking can make good pickles or be stuffed if the seeds are removed). If cucumbers are left to mature on the vines, fewer flowers will develop.

Adequate moisture is essential, and you can quickly see the difference in the yellow leaves and misshapen fruit that develop when cucumber roots are crying for water. Unless they get it, the plant will become embittered, then simply cease to produce until it gets a good rain. This basic need of cucumbers should be obvious to the cook who recognizes that cucumbers are largely composed of water—that is why they are both low in calories and highly refreshing.

Cucumbers are usually eaten raw or pickled, but they may also be served as a hot vegetable. This is a good way to use cucumbers that have grown large and seedy, because the seeds are removed

Cucumbers and the Moon

The old wives' tale that vine plants are most productive during the full moon really seems to be true. I've noticed that an abundance of fruit develops right after the full moon. I suspect it might have something to do with the extra activity of night moths and other insects that pollinated the flowers on those nights four weeks earlier.

before cooking. When using older ones, you will need fewer and the cooking time will be longer.

○*Cucumbers with Cream Sauce*

These cucumbers are especially good with fish.

6 cucumbers (6 inches long)	2 tablespoons butter
Salt	White pepper
1 cup milk	2 teaspoons chopped fresh dill or
1 tablespoon flour	chervil or 1 teaspoon dried

Pare the cucumbers, cut into quarters lengthwise, and remove seeds. Let soak in cold water for 30 minutes. Then cut into chunks and put in a pan, cover with boiling water, add ½ teaspoon salt, and boil until tender (about 15 minutes). Drain and chop into smaller pieces.

Make a cream sauce with flour, butter, and milk seasoned with salt and white pepper. Add dill or chervil. Pour over the cucumbers and serve. *Serves 6.*

○*Braised Cucumbers*

This old-fashioned recipe, from Mrs. S. T. Rorer's *How to Cook Vegetables* (1892), makes a light meal when served on squares of buttered toast.

6 cucumbers (6-8 inches long)	1 tablespoon flour
1 tablespoon butter	1 cup chicken stock
1 small onion, peeled and chopped	Salt and pepper

Pare the cucumbers, cut into quarters lengthwise, and remove seeds. Melt butter in a fry pan, add the onion, and cook until golden. Then add the strips of cucumber and turn carefully until they are a light brown. Remove from pan with a pancake turner. Stir flour into fry pan and then add the stock, stirring constantly until it boils. Season to taste. Return cucumbers to pan, cover, and braise gently 20 minutes. ***Serves 4.***

° Cucumbers with Lemon Butter and Dill

Hollandaise sauce may be substituted for the butter sauce. These cucumbers are good with fish or ham.

4 cucumbers (1½ inches in
   diameter)
1 cup water
½ teaspoon celery salt
¼ cup butter

1 tablespoon lemon juice
1 tablespoon finely chopped fresh
   dillweed or 1 teaspoon dried
2 tablespoons seasoned bread
   crumbs

Peel the cucumbers and cut in quarters lengthwise. Cook in water seasoned with celery salt until tender but still a bit crisp. Melt butter and add lemon juice and dill. Place cooked cucumber strips on a platter. Sprinkle crumbs over them and pour butter sauce over all.

Serves 4.

Other Ideas for Cucumbers

- ° Make a cucumber sauce for fish by finely dicing cucumbers and folding them into sour cream or yogurt.
- ° Use cucumbers in sandwiches, adding watercress or thinly sliced onions.
- ° Shred or julienne cucumbers, toss with vinegar, drain, and mound on a salad platter or use as a garnish.
- ° Layer thinly sliced cucumbers, green peppers, onions, and zucchini and marinate in vinaigrette.
- ° Make a Greek salad with chopped cucumbers, feta cheese, olives, chopped fresh mint, lemon juice, and oil.
- ° Add minced cucumbers and dill to yogurt to make a refreshing soup.
- ° Stuff cucumbers as you would zucchini: scoop out seeds, blanch cucumbers for a few minutes, fill with your favorite stuffing, and bake at 350° F. for about 30 minutes.
- ° Add cucumbers to gazpacho, the spicy cold fresh tomato soup that incorporates so many good things from the garden.
- ° Toss chopped cucumbers with cold pasta, chives, mint or savory, oil, vinegar, and lots of freshly ground pepper.

You may wonder why a large purple vegetable got to be called eggplant. It's because the eggplants growing in Asia hundreds of years ago produced white fruits as small as eggs. They were introduced to Europe by way of China and India, where they are a very popular vegetable.

Most eggplants used today are the purple varieties, and they differ in size and shape. They need to be started indoors about eight weeks before the last frost date in your area and then set out in rich, warm soil. Eggplant needs lots of water, and varieties with large fruit may need staking. Rabbits leave the plants alone, but not the small black flea beetles which arrive in June. They can turn the leaves to lace in two nights if plants are not protected by rotenone.

Because it is the seeds of eggplant that have the strong flavor, it is best to use it when young, not more than 3 inches in diameter. You can't pull an eggplant off the plant. The tough stem has to be cut.

I think one has to cultivate a taste for eggplant. I hated it as a child, but like it now. It has to be well cooked to bring out its real flavor. Eggplant discolors in air; do not cut or peel it ahead of time. Some cooks sprinkle it with salt and let it "weep" out excess water for about half an hour. Its cousin the tomato is a good accompaniment for eggplant, and onions and olive oil bring out its flavor. It goes well with fish, lamb, and pork.

○ *Fried Eggplant*

Fried eggplant, macaroni and cheese, and a platter of sliced tomatoes are one of my favorite combinations for a meal.

2 young eggplants (2½ inches across)	Bread or cracker crumbs
1 egg beaten lightly with 1 tablespoon hot water	Oil for fry pan

Slice unpeeled eggplant ½ inch thick or less. Dip in egg, then in crumbs, and put slices into a frying pan with hot oil just covering the bottom. (Eggplant has the characteristic of absorbing oil, so use just enough to brown the slices.) Turn the slices over when brown and cook the other side. Drain on brown paper. Add more oil to the pan as you cook remaining slices. Salt just before serving.   *Serves 3.*

○ *Scorched Eggplant*

For this Indian dish, put one large or two small eggplants—about 2 pounds—on a pan about 8 inches from the broiler. Turn broiler on and, as eggplant scorches, keep turning it over until skin is all brown. Then turn broiler off and bake eggplant in 375° oven until it is soft. Remove from oven and scrape off scorched skin with a blunt knife.

Sauté 2 chopped onions in a fry pan until light brown. Mash the eggplant and add it to onions in the pan. Season with a good pinch of turmeric, 1 tablespoon sesame seed, ½ teaspoon ground coriander, and salt and pepper to taste. You might want to squeeze lemon on it, but the Indians do not.   *Serves 3-4.*

Other Ideas for Eggplant

○ Eggplant can be rather bland. Perk it up with herbs—basil, oregano, savory, sage, or thyme—or spices such as cumin, nutmeg, chili powder.

○ Marinate 1½-inch cubes of eggplant in an oil dressing and use when making shish kebabs.

- To stuff eggplants, halve them, scoop out the pulp (leave a ¾-inch-thick shell), and sauté it with ground meat. Add tomato sauce and herbs, fill eggplant shells with mixture, place in greased pan, cover with foil, and bake 40 minutes at 400° F.
- Cut eggplant into fingers, dip in beaten egg, roll in crumbs, and deep-fry in hot oil.
- For poor man's caviar, bake a large eggplant at 400° F. for 1 hour. Peel, chop, and sauté with minced onion, green pepper, and garlic. Add some chopped tomato if you like. Season to taste with salt, pepper, and lemon juice, simmer until thick, then chill.
- Sauté tomatoes, eggplant, zucchini, onions, garlic, and peppers in olive oil until almost puréed and dry. Eat as is, or spread on a crust and top with cheese for pizza.
- Make vegetarian eggplant curry by simmering cubed eggplant with green peppers, potatoes, garlic, and curry powder. Stir in tomato wedges or yogurt if you like.
- Fill pita or pocket bread with hot eggplant mixtures for an informal hot lunch.
- It is claimed that the Arabs know a thousand ways to prepare eggplant—look in Middle Eastern cookbooks for other ideas. See also Eggplant and Rice Casserole and Eggplant Dip.

Mid~
Summer
Greens

An American missionary working in southwestern China found the first odorless marigold in the 1930s and told my husband about it. He bought the seeds the missionary had collected, and a great bond grew between the two men. Mr. Burpee was always looking for "new" plants to introduce to gardeners. It was easier to find or "create" new flowers than new vegetables. So he asked this missionary if he would look for vegetables that American gardeners could grow in their gardens. The missionary sent seeds of many Oriental vegetables new to American gardens—among them a great assortment of turnip-type plants, tampala, and Malabar spinach.

Tampala

Tampala is a horticultural variety of *Amaranthus gangeticus.* This particular variety, selected from among many grown in Asia, was introduced to American gardeners commercially by David Burpee in 1945. Its importance for American gardens is that it is a "greens" which will grow in hot weather.

The seeds are sown in the garden in June, and in forty-five days young plants are ready to use. I like its upright bushy plant habit—the leaves stay cleaner than spinach. When growing for quantity processing, the plants are cut when about eight inches tall. Thin out the plants, allowing eight to ten inches between those left to grow to a mature size. Unfortunately, there is a root rot that suddenly attacks all varieties of *Amaranthus* in late summer after a hot, wet spell, so it is best to enjoy tampala while you have it. Pick tampala in the morning while the leaves are turgid.

The flavor of tampala is mild, not metallic like spinach, and the texture is drier, since it has twice the solids of spinach. It has considerably more protein and calcium than spinach and about the same amount of iron, though not as much vitamin B or C. The leaves are not fleshy and wilt quickly, so I do not recommend it for salads, but it freezes well.

When preparing plants for cooking, just wash and cut them across so they won't be stringy. If using old plants, I suggest stripping off the leaves, cutting the stems in one-inch lengths, and cooking them eight to ten minutes before adding the leaves. It takes longer to cook tampala than spinach, but it can be substituted for spinach in many recipes (see ideas in discussion of spinach).

∘ *Tampala with Hot Bacon Dressing*

6 strips bacon	1 teaspoon salt
½ cup sugar	½ cup water
2 tablespoons flour	½ cup vinegar
1 tablespoon lemon juice	1 pound tampala, cleaned and sliced

Fry bacon until crisp, drain off fat, reserving ¼ cup. Crumble bacon and set aside. Mix sugar and flour and add to lemon juice, salt, water, vinegar, and bacon fat. Cook in top of a double boiler for 7 minutes, until smooth. Add half the crumbled bacon.

Put tampala into a large pan and toss 4 or 5 times with the hot bacon dressing over medium heat for 5 minutes. Serve at once, using rest of crumbled bacon as a garnish. **Serves 6.**

° *Tampala Cheese Soufflé*

1 teaspoon chopped onion	¾ teaspoon salt
2 tablespoons fat	⅛ teaspoon pepper
2 tablespoons flour	3 eggs, separated
½ cup milk	1 cup chopped cooked tampala,
¼ cup grated cheese	well drained

Sauté onion in fat until slightly yellow. Stir in flour and gradually add milk. Cook, stirring constantly, until thickened. Add cheese, salt, and pepper. Place over hot water in double boiler; stir until cheese melts. Beat the egg yolks well and add with tampala to cheese sauce, then fold in stiffly beaten egg whites. Turn the mixture into a greased casserole and set in a pan of hot water. Bake in a 350° oven for about 50 minutes. *Serves 4.*

° *Tampala Ring*

Garnish this attractive ring with bacon curls and mushrooms if you wish.

4 cups cooked tampala	3 cups cooked carrots and celery in
4 tablespoons butter	cream sauce, or creamed
¾ teaspoon salt	chicken, turkey, or hard-boiled
	eggs for filling

Drain tampala thoroughly. Chop fine and season with butter and salt. Press firmly into greased ring mold and place in a 250° oven for 20 minutes. Unmold ring onto plate and fill the center with creamed filling of your choice. *Serves 6.*

Malabar Spinach

Malabar spinach, a plant from India, is a climbing vine that grows only in hot weather. I am told that the Indians often let the plants grow over their huts. The vines do not have tendrils, so they spread over the ground unless tied to a support. Malabar spinach can be grown in a greenhouse in the winter. The flowers are very small pink knobs in the axils of the leaves. The stems are one-quarter of an inch or more across, and the leaves resemble large spinach leaves but are very shiny and thick. The flavor is similar to New Zealand spinach but not as strong. Some people add Malabar leaves to salads, but I'm not fond of their raw flavor. The tips of the runners are tender and a bit like asparagus in appearance and flavor; they can be prepared the same way.

Malabar leaves do not boil down as much as spinach. Wash the leaves and cut them across with scissors. Put in a large pot, add a scant teaspoon of salt (less if you plan to use undiluted soup for seasoning), and pour boiling water over to cover. Cook for only five minutes on high heat. The greens become gummy if overcooked. Drain and chop finer if you wish. Mix with your favorite cream sauce or heated undiluted canned cream of celery or mushroom soup. Or add lightly browned chopped onion, butter, and a little lemon juice.

The leaves can also be cooked in the Oriental way of wilting and steaming in a fry pan in which onion has been browned in oil. Leave the onion in the pan. Squeeze lemon juice onto the spinach before serving.

To cook Malabar spinach tips, cut eight-inch lengths from the tips of the runners. Leave the youngest leaves on the tips of the stems. Cook flat in salted boiling water until tender but not floppy, about eight minutes, depending on quantity. Serve with hollandaise sauce or lemon butter.

New Zealand Spinach

This is an excellent midsummer-through-fall boiling green. The plant forms a spreading mat a foot long in the garden. It has many branches bearing brittle, fleshy leaves.

Though it is a native of Southeast Asia and New Zealand, it is not hurt by a light frost and can be used into November if you protect it with a drop cloth or burlap. However, late in the season hard seeds develop in the axils of the leaves, and these have to be nipped off before cooking. New Zealand spinach will self-sow if given the chance. The seeds remain dormant in the soil until spring, and young plants appear in late May if you do not disturb the soil. However, if you are planting fresh seed, wait until the soil has warmed up.

The seeds in the packet are like small, hard black nuts but each nut contains four smaller seeds. Usually only one grows. As the shell is very hard, to hasten germination it is best to soak the seeds overnight. Sow them directly in the garden four to six inches apart. They will take about three weeks to germinate in warm weather when given plenty of water. As the plants grow, thin to a foot apart.

New Zealand spinach is trouble-free—no bugs like it. The more it is picked the more it produces. It has one big advantage over regular spinach: the leaves are clean and require very little washing. Pick the ends of the growing branches—about three or four inches long. Use both stems and leaves. If leaves alone are used, I find the flavor a bit too strong. Cook and serve the same way you do chard or spinach (see ideas where they are discussed). A mixture of chard and New Zealand spinach has a very nice flavor.

Okra, a favorite vegetable of southerners, is a hot-weather crop. Seeds are sown directly in the garden, though some northerners start them indoors. Okra is a bushy plant that needs space—thin seedlings to at least two feet apart. The plants are usually two to four feet tall (Emerald okra, however, grows to six or seven feet) with pretty flowers like hollyhocks that start low on the stem.

Two weeks after the blossoms fade, look for the okra pods, which grow quickly and are best when thumb length. When too old they become stringy. If in doubt, test with your thumbnail. If you can pierce a ridge of the pod, it's okay. Older okra can be used to flavor soups; even the seeds give flavor.

Okra has a clear gummy sap that gives it an unpleasant texture when it is not handled or cooked properly. It is best not to bruise the pods, so take clippers to the garden. I gather mine as they develop and store them dry in a plastic bag in the refrigerator until I have enough for a meal or for the freezer. Before freezing, plunge whole okra into boiling water for 1 minute, then cool immediately under cold running water. Dry on paper towels, put in freezer bags, squeeze air out, and tie as you would a balloon.

Do not use copper, brass, iron, or tin utensils with okra—they will discolor it—and do not overcook okra lest it become slimy. Okra is most commonly used as a vegetable in soup, particularly gumbo. My favorite way to serve it is in stewed tomatoes.

⌐*Okra in Stewed Tomatoes*

2 cups fresh stewed or canned
  tomatoes
6-8 small okra
¼ teaspoon salt

½ teaspoon sugar
1 teaspoon seasoned bread crumbs
  (optional)
1 teaspoon butter, optional

Heat the tomatoes. Cut off the stems and tips of the okra and slice ½ inch thick. Add to the hot tomatoes and simmer 8–10 minutes, no longer. To keep the okra green, do not cover the pot. Add salt and sugar after tasting. If you wish to thicken the mixture, add bread crumbs. A teaspoon of butter gives it a nice glow.   *Serves 4-5.*

○Oven-Fried Okra

Cut pods across in ¼-inch slices. Put salted cornmeal or white or whole-wheat flour in a paper bag, add some of the okra, and shake the bag. Spread floured slices on a buttered cookie sheet, dot with butter, and bake at 375° F. for 30 minutes. Stir once or twice.

○Okra Fry Covered with Corn

This recipe is taken from Mrs. Rorer's *How to Cook Vegetables* (published by W. Atlee Burpee Company, 1892).

2 tablespoons bacon fat	2 tablespoons flour
2 cups sliced okra	1 cup milk
1 slice onion	1 teaspoon salt
Corn scraped from 12 ears	Pepper

Put the bacon fat in a fry pan and cook the okra with onion until nicely browned. Add the corn, stir, and watch carefully until thoroughly cooked, about 10 minutes. Push the corn and okra mixture to one side. Stir in the flour and mix in the milk, stirring constantly until boiling. Add salt and a dash of pepper. Mix all together. Serve very hot.   *Serves 6.*

○Stuffed Okra

Believe me, you can have fun with okra as a hot canapé or a side dish—and be original too!

Use about 6 okra pods no more than 3–4 inches; they should be tender enough for your finger nail to cut across a rib. Leave on ⅓ inch of stem. Wash gently and cut in half lengthwise. Cut out pithy center to make a cavity for the filling. Do not remove the seeds. Dip okra in 1 egg beaten with 1 tablespoon cold water.

Spread the cut sides with a filling of soft cheese or a mixture of cream cheese and barbecue sauce. The filling can be anything else you have around that is moist, such as a clam or other cocktail spread.

Roll the okra in ⅓ cup cornmeal seasoned with ½ teaspoon salt. Place a piece of foil on a baking sheet and turn the edges up. Pour 2 tablespoons oil on foil. Place okra cut side up on the foil and spoon a little oil on top. Bake in a 400° oven for 15 minutes. **Serves 4.**

Other Ideas for Okra

○ Onions, green pepper, and lemon juice are good flavoring for okra. Suitable herbs are oregano, thyme, marjoram, and basil.

○ For okra salad, boil pods (with stems left on) until barely tender, drain, and chill. Serve with vinaigrette or a dip, using stems as handles when dipping in dressing.

○ For fried okra, wash and dry okra pods, cut in half lengthwise, roll in salted cornmeal, and fry in deep fat until golden brown.

○ Okra goes well with eggplant: simmer them together with onion and chopped ripe tomatoes.

○ Serve okra soup-stews over fluffy white rice to soak up the juices.

○ In Trinidad, thinly sliced okra is cooked with cornmeal, water, oregano, and butter to make a thick mixture that is pressed into a buttered mold, then unmolded and sliced like cake— delicious with a spicy tomato sauce.

○ Make tender-crisp okra pickles with very young pods. In each of 6 pint jars put ⅛ teaspoon red pepper flakes, half a garlic clove, and ½ teaspoon mustard seeds. Using 2 pounds okra, fill the jars. Bring 4 cups vinegar, 2 cups water, and 5 tablespoons coarse salt to a boil and pour over okra in jars.

Onions are one of the oldest recorded vegetables and the most universally used. Onion is added to more dishes than any other seasoning except salt.

Green onions, scallions, or spring onions are often the first crop from the garden. They can be grown from onion sets that look like tiny onions (which they are) or planted as seeds and pulled up before the onion bulb has had a chance to mature.

The Evergreen Long White Bunching or Japanese bunching onions do not produce bulbs but clumps of green onions that grow like chives. They are thinner than scallions grown from sets, but with them you can have nice green onions in the fall and very early the next spring. They are perennial but do need some protection, such as tree leaves, in northern winters.

It would be nice if onion sets were sold from a bin so we could select firm little bulblets a half inch across or smaller, but usually they are not. So, when I get my sets, I sort them out and separate the larger ones from the smaller ones.

Though onion sets are supposed to be immature onions which have not developed enough to produce a flower, often those sets that are larger than a dime have matured a bit too much. When they are planted they will produce a one-sided onion and a tough flower stalk beside it. So I use these larger ones for scallions rather than allow them to mature.

I plant sets in the garden as soon as the soil is dry enough to crumble. It doesn't matter if snow falls on them (a late spring snow is sometimes called an onion snow).

Make a furrow three inches deep in the garden and scatter a lawn fertilizer in the bottom. Where you want to grow scallions, fill the furrow with earth up to one inch from the top and plant the larger onion sets two inches apart. They should be just covered with earth. Label this part of the row "scallions," and be sure to use them as they grow.

Let smaller sets develop into mature onions. They should be planted two inches deep and four inches apart in the furrow to give the bulbs space in which to grow. Label this section of the row "onions."

The best winter-keeping onions, such as Southport Yellow Globe, are those grown from seeds planted in seed beds in a cold frame or a flat indoors in late spring. The seedlings look like grass wearing a black hat (which is the seed coat). They are very thin and will bend over as they grow taller, so cut them back to a height of 3–4 inches until they are thick enough to handle easily when transplanting to the garden. Follow directions on the seed packets.

There is a much greater choice in varieties of onions grown from seeds than from sets. Read the descriptions of onions carefully when selecting seeds. Some varieties, such as Yellow Bermuda, grow best in the South, and the large slicing onions need light soil. Some white onions are not good keepers but are especially sweet, as is the giant red onion.

Other members of the onion family that are worthwhile to grow are leeks (discussed elsewhere), chives (see herbs), shallots, and garlic. Delicate shallots, with their mild but distinct flavor, grow in a cluster of bulbs attached at the base. Separate the bulblets

Garlic Sauce

For garlic sauce (aïoli), delicious on crusty bread, in soup, or as a dip, place 5 garlic cloves in the blender, add ¼ cup olive oil, 3 egg yolks, and 3 tablespoons lemon juice, and blend until garlic is smooth. Gradually add ¾ cup oil—sauce will become creamy.

and plant like onion sets. (Often people who have an allergic reaction to onions can eat shallots.) Pungent garlic has many small sections (cloves) that are separated and planted tip upward. Elephant garlic develops into bulbs with large cloves that have a milder flavor than regular garlic. Since both shallots and garlic are expensive in the market, they are profitably grown by lovers of well-seasoned food.

Onions require more fertilizer and especially nitrogen than most garden vegetables. If in your past experience most of the onions have produced flowers, it is an indication of insufficient nitrogen. This happens sometimes when a lot of dried leaves have been worked into the soil, because the bacteria that decay the leaves are also nitrogen feeders. I fertilize onions two or three times during the growing season, depending on how heavy the rains have been. Onions also need adequate water and will become pungent if not kept moist.

Onions can be pulled as soon as they are large enough to use, but when their leaves turn brown and limp, they must be harvested. If left in the ground longer, they will start to rot. I take up my onions in late July or early August. Dig them when the ground is dry so the earth will shake off. Spread them out in some airy place where they will not get wet. When the roots and leaves have dried, clean them off and store in a mesh bag hung in a dry place.

When peeling or cutting onions it is best to use a really sharp knife—it prevents the juice from squirting so much and bringing tears. When preparing a lot of onions I put on the kitchen vent fan and work with the onions between me and the fan. Some people find a food processor useful for chopping and slicing onions.

I often add a little chopped raw onion to soups and creamed vegetables just before serving. Instead of getting out my chopper, I cut a fine grid across a whole onion to a depth of one or two slices, then cut as for a slice, and I have nice little crumbly cubes ready to add and usually no tears.

There are several tricks to keeping onions whole when cooking them as a vegetable. The only sure-fire one is a toothpick pushed through across the bulb, but some other helps are to cut a cross one-half inch deep into the stem end or poke two holes through the side of the onion. This works if the holes are as large as an ice pick. It is the expanding air in an onion that pushes the center out.

Whole onions are often added to stews or braised dishes. I like them especially cooked along with a lamb roast. Boiled onions have been considered a good cure for a cold. Once I was fed them for three days when away from home at a small British boarding school in Palestine—so they are not one of my favorite vegetables. But a casserole of boiled onions in a tasty cream sauce flavored with tarragon, dill, or cheese can be very good.

◦ Stuffed Onions

This recipe is taken from Mrs. S. T. Rorer's *How to Cook Vegetables*. It is an unexpected dish, good for a luncheon.

Boil six large onions without peeling for 45 minutes. Drain, remove the skins, and with a sharp knife cut out the center of each. Mix a cup of finely chopped ham or tongue with ½ cup bread crumbs, 2 tablespoons cream, a dash of pepper or mustard, and 2 tablespoons melted butter.

Fill the onions with this mixture. Place in a baking pan and baste with more melted butter. Dust with more bread crumbs and bake in a 300° oven for 45–60 minutes. Serve with a cream sauce.

Other Ideas for Onions

- When using onions in salads, I like to have the pieces identifiable so that if there is too much onion for someone's taste, it can be put to one side. I cut onions for salad in crescents about 1 inch long.
- For raw-onion lovers, make a simple but pretty salad by marinating sweet white and red onion rings in vinaigrette with lots of fresh herbs: parsley, mint, dill, or chives.
- Use yellow Spanish onions for onion soup—their sugar caramelizes with long, slow sautéing and produces the exquisite flavor and rich color of a good onion soup.
- Dropping onion rings in ice water to chill crisps them and makes them milder.

- Even after onions have developed, the green leaves are good to add to soups for flavor and color and also as a cooked green vegetable. Wash and cut the onion leaves across into 1-inch lengths and stir-fry in oil or butter, then simmer on low heat, covered, for 10 minutes.
- Make the wonderful French soubise by braising about 2 pounds of thinly sliced onions with ½ cup rice in butter in a slow oven until rice is very soft and onions have dissolved in their own juices. Eat as is, thin with cream and season for soup, or make into a cream sauce.
- Add unpeeled onions to the stockpot—the skins will add color. Or save onion peels and add them to water for hard-boiled eggs to dye them yellow for Easter. Children will enjoy another method: Wrap each egg in a husk of onion peels and enclose in a cheesecloth bag. Hard-boil eggs, then unwrap—they will be mottled or marbled, beautiful when rubbed with a little oil.
- Sauté lots of sliced onions with strips of green pepper and use to top sweet or hot Italian sausages. Or add the onions and peppers to corn for a vegetable dish.
- Pickle shallots in a light vinegar (rice wine vinegar is good) with tarragon or pickling spices.

Peppers are native to tropical America. They are pretty plants, especially when the fruits ripen to red against the dark green foliage. They are also full of vitamins. And they are very useful. Even if I did not have a vegetable garden I would be sure to plant a few sweet pepper plants somewhere, since so many dishes are improved by adding fresh peppers.

The seed for peppers is usually started indoors. They germinate only in a warm atmosphere and do not like too much moisture until they are growing well. Before the plants are set out, all danger of frost should be past and the plants should be about eight inches tall. Space plants two to three feet apart. In areas where there are lots of birds, I advise protecting the plants—birds love to nip the tops of young pepper plants. To protect them, I use Hotkaps, which I cut open at the top to let in light, air, and rain. Peppers have a shallow root system, so they like the support of a stake as they develop. As green peppers ripen and turn red, the flavor becomes sweeter.

I grow different varieties for different uses. Regular bell peppers are good to stuff, put in salads, and use in Italian dishes. For cocktail-party snacks, Sweet Banana peppers really get attention. I slice them lengthwise and fill with a favorite spread or use with a dip. They are also tasty braised. Sweet Cherry peppers are another good finger food.

I enjoy the flavor of Burpee's Early Pimento most of all, and I think it is the best variety for freezing. To freeze peppers, I quarter them lengthwise, remove the seeds, peel off the skin with a swivel peeler, wrap each piece separately in plastic wrap, and put them in a freezer bag.

Unfortunately, peppers are not easily digested, but I find that peeling them helps. That's why I select smooth, thick-fleshed varieties like pimento and Yolo Wonder. You can also roast them to aid peeling and produce a sweet, rich flavor: impale the whole pepper on a skewer and turn it over a gas flame until it is charred and blistered, then pull off the skin. Or char the peppers under the broiler, seal them in a brown paper bag for fifteen minutes, and slip off the skins. Remove seeds and membranes, whose flavor is sharp—if peppers still have too assertive a flavor, parboiling reduces its strength.

Hot peppers are used in Latin American, Oriental, and Indian dishes. Like other peppers, they freeze very well, but I prefer to dry hot peppers. It's fun to have one or two hot pepper plants for their beauty but also for the snap they can give to a mixed dish or to pickles. I like the surprise of a little bit of hot pepper now and then. Remember the seeds and veins are the hottest part.

◦ *Stuffed Peppers*

Stuffing is an excellent way to use leftover meats and vegetables.

4 peppers	**½ cup leftover cooked rice**
¼ cup chopped onions	**1 tablespoon snipped parsley**
¼ cup chopped celery	**2 teaspoons Worcestershire sauce**
1 teaspoon oil	**1 cup tomato sauce**
½ cup leftover cooked beef,	**Grated Parmesan cheese**
chopped	

Cut off the stem ends of the peppers and take out the seeds. Cook peppers whole in boiling water for 5 minutes, then drain. Lightly brown onions and celery in oil. Combine with meat, rice, parsley, and Worcestershire sauce. Stuff peppers, put in a deep baking dish, and pour tomato sauce around them. Sprinkle Parmesan cheese on top and bake at 350° F. for 45 minutes.   *Serves 4.*

Variations: If you have any leftover creamed corn, even ½ cup will add flavor, or add leftover carrots or beans. Substitute chopped shrimp or ham for ground meat, or use corned-beef hash spiked with ketchup, oregano, and minced scallions.

Other Ideas for Peppers

- ◦ I use peppers mostly for the flavor and color they add to dishes, especially creamed chicken or turkey. A little chopped sautéed pepper can perk up many other dishes: macaroni and cheese, omelets, frittate, rice, and pizza.
- ◦ As hors d'oeuvre, strips of peppers are so colorful—red, yellow, orange, and green—that they can make a beautiful arrangement on the buffet table. Use in place of chips with a dip.
- ◦ For an attractive addition to a salad platter, pack a small pepper with softened cream cheese (flavored if you like). Chill thoroughly, then cut crosswise into thin slices.
- ◦ Sauté sweet pepper strips in olive oil with onions and garlic. Use hot to top Italian sausages in rolls or sprinkle with vinegar and chill to serve as a salad.

- Make hot pepper sauce with minced hot peppers, finely chopped onion and tomatoes, vinegar, sugar, and salt. Simmer until thick, adjusting amounts to your taste.
- The "hot" sap of hot peppers will burn your fingertips if you handle them a lot, and it takes several washings with soap and water to get it off.
- Stir-fry strips of red and green sweet peppers with strips of onion and steak.
- Pickle sweet pepper strips or chunks or whole sweet cherry peppers with sliced onions in your favorite pickling brine.
- Make your own "canned" pimentos by making lengthwise cuts in fresh pimentos and carefully removing seeds and pith. Pack in 8-ounce canning jars and pour a light salt brine over them—½ teaspoon salt to a pint of water. Close jars just tight enough to keep water out, as some air must get out. Process in hot water covering the jars for 40 minutes after the water has come to a boil. Tighten lids as each jar is removed from the hot water.
- A most attractive table decoration can be made with an assortment of fresh sweet peppers at different stages of ripeness. They are so bright and colorful.

It is no wonder that squashes grow well in gardens in the United States—they are native to the American continent. In Central America, the squash can be dated back to prehistory; it was cultivated by

Mexicans for its flesh and seeds in 5000 B.C., and even our word for the vegetable comes from the Narragansett *askutasquash*.

There are several types of summer squash, and each has its characteristics in the garden and for cooking. All summer squashes are prolific, quick-growing vegetables. The more often they are picked, the more fruit the plants will produce.

Squash should be planted directly in the garden as soon as the ground is really warm, with no likelihood of frost. I plant a cluster of three to four seeds, three feet apart in a row, and when the seedlings are up, thin to two plants. I leave two plants just for precaution and, when the plants are no longer tempting to birds and cutworms, thin to one plant.

All squash, even the bush types, need room to grow. The more light and air the plants have the healthier they will be. They also need fairly rich soil and a constant supply of water to their roots. A mulch is helpful for holding moisture and keeping fruit off the ground. If you pick the fruits just as soon as they are the size you want, for a family of four you will not need many plants of any one variety: at most, three early golden, three white bush, and two zucchini (actually, when zucchini bears as heavily as it is wont to, one plant seems like enough to feed the neighborhood).

Insects and wilt disease can be a problem for summer squash. If a squash plant becomes infected and starts to wilt, pull it out and discard it so the disease won't spread. If your first planting succumbs, make a second planting in another part of the garden.

I have heard that the squash beetle likes to lay its eggs in a dark place. One way to deter these pests is to put some light-reflecting material around the base of each plant. I have had some good luck by placing shiny aluminum pie plates under the plants.

All summer squash varieties are good just steamed and served with butter. Younger squash are the greater delicacy, but there are many uses for the large, fully mature fruits.

Yellow Crookneck and Straightneck Squash

Early yellow crooknecks are a good early-season squash, with more flavor, I think, than zucchini, but the plants tend to die back in hot, humid weather.

These squashes must be used young while the skin is tender because the skin has the flavor. Wash, slice, and stir-fry in oil just before sitting down at the table. Go easy on salt, and add either chopped parsley or chives. You may also use chopped red pepper if you have it in your freezer (bell peppers are usually not ripe as soon as this squash is available). See also recipe for Yellow Corn and Squash Frittata.

White Bush, Patty Pan, or Scalloped Squash

These are the least tasty of all summer squash—they should not be used randomly in squash recipes. You must continually pick them to keep the plants bearing. The charm of white bush squash is two-fold: when it is small (1½ inches in diameter), you can dip it in batter and fry it whole; larger fruits can be scooped out, parboiled, stuffed with vegetable or meat fillings, and baked—they make attractive individual servings and are a good way to use leftovers. Or try this delicate filling that complements the mild flavor of white patty pans:

○ Stuffed White Squash

6 small patty pan squash
8 ounces cream cheese, at room
  temperature
1 tablespoon cream, sour cream, or
  milk
2 scallions or shallots, minced

1 teaspoon minced parsley
Salt and white pepper to taste
Paprika to taste

Parboil the whole squashes for about 10 minutes or until barely tender. Scoop out the centers, then mix this pulp thoroughly with remaining ingredients and fill the shells. Place in a greased baking pan, pour in water just to cover bottom, and bake at 350° F. for 20 minutes.   *Serves 6.*

Green Zucchini Squash

Zucchini are long and green (except for yellow zucchini) and contain a lot of water when young, but they get firmer, then pulpy, when old. They quickly grow beyond the 8-inch length, after which they are not as flavorful. The plants are very prolific if the squashes are kept picked. Zucchini requires no peeling or seeding and therefore is very quick and easy to prepare. Although recipes are a dime a dozen for this popular squash, these are my favorites.

° *Zucchini Squash Salad*

Firm green lettuce (such as
  romaine or Fordhook)
Sliced young zucchini
Sliced cucumbers
¼ cup vinegar
2 tablespoons water
½ teaspoon dried oregano

½ teaspoon cumin
1 teaspoon salt
3 drops Tabasco
1 teaspoon sugar
2 tablespoons chopped fresh
  chives or 1 tablespoon dried
1 cup vegetable oil

Break lettuce into small bits. Add an equal quantity of sliced zucchini and one-third as much sliced cucumbers. Simmer vinegar, water, oregano, and cumin 10 minutes to bring out flavors. Cool. Add remaining ingredients and toss with greens.

° *Broiled Zucchini*

Allow one 6–8-inch zucchini per person. Wash, drop into enough boiling salted water to cover, and simmer for 5 minutes. Lift from the water and cut in half lengthwise. Arrange on a broiling pan, placing cut surfaces up. Score the tops with a sharp knife and coat lightly with butter. Sprinkle with celery salt, then with seasoned bread crumbs, and finally grated Parmesan cheese. Dot with butter and place under a preheated broiler for a few minutes, or until lightly browned over entire top surface.

◦ *Sautéed Zucchini with Herbs*

3 tablespoons butter or vegetable
  oil
½ yellow onion, chopped fine
1½ teaspoons chopped fresh
  marjoram, or 2 teaspoons
  snipped fresh dill, or ½ teaspoon
  cumin seed

1 pound small unpeeled zucchini,
  sliced thin
½ teaspoon salt

Heat the butter or oil in a large, heavy skillet. Add the onion and brown lightly over high heat. Mix the herb of your choice with the zucchini. Add to the skillet and stir-fry for 1 minute. Cover with a spatter lid. Reduce heat and simmer for 5 minutes. Sprinkle with salt just before serving.   *Serves 4.*

◦ *Zucchini Fritters*

This is a way to use large zucchini, which have a lower water content.

3 cups coarsely grated zucchini
1 cup biscuit mix
½ cup grated sharp cheese
1 egg, slightly beaten

1 tablespoon chopped parsley or
  chives
1 clove garlic, chopped
Salt and pepper to taste, or 3 drops
  Tabasco
Oil

Mix all ingredients (except oil) together and drop from spoon into pan of hot oil, ¼–½ inch deep. Turn when first side is brown. Drain on brown paper in warm oven until all fritters are ready to serve.

Serves 4.

◦ *Zucchini, Cheese, and Herb Muffins*

This recipe is by Joan Thomsen. My variation is to substitute ¼ cup crumbled bacon for the cheeses, and add 2 teaspoons pepper relish.

3 cups flour
1 cup shredded zucchini
⅓ cup sugar
3 tablespoons grated Parmesan
  cheese
¼ cup grated sharp cheese
5 teaspoons baking powder
½ teaspoon baking soda

1½ teaspoons salt
¼ teaspoon marjoram
3 tablespoons chopped parsley
⅓ cup butter or margarine
1 cup buttermilk (see note)
2 eggs
¼ cup grated onion

Mix together the flour, zucchini, sugar, cheeses, baking powder, baking soda, salt, marjoram, and parsley. Melt butter or margarine, stir in buttermilk, eggs, and onion, and stir until smooth. Stir into flour mixture until just blended (mixture may seem dry). Drop by spoonfuls into greased muffin pans, filling each about half full. Bake muffins in a 350° oven for 15 minutes for small, 25 minutes for 2-inch muffin cups. (Or spread mixture in a greased 9x5x3-inch pan and bake 55–60 minutes.) *Makes about 30 small muffins.*

Note: If you don't have buttermilk, measure 2 tablespoons vinegar into a cup and add milk to make 1 cup.

Golden Zucchini

These are less watery than green varieties and must be used only when young. They can be cooked the same as green zucchini, but I like to do something different with them featuring their color. Use some chopped ripe red peppers with them for color contrast and flavor.

◦ *Golden Zucchini à la Krishna*

This dish was created to serve to Craig Claiborne as part of a vegetable luncheon and he named it.

2 medium-size golden zucchini
  (about 1¼ pounds)
Salt
1 large carrot (about ¼ pound),
  peeled
2 tablespoons butter
2 tablespoons flour
½ teaspoon curry powder
½ teaspoon chopped fresh fennel
  leaves or fennel seeds

1 cup milk
Freshly ground pepper to taste
1 tablespoon chopped sweet red
  pepper
1 tablespoon bread crumbs
1 teaspoon grated Parmesan cheese
½ teaspoon paprika
Butter (optional)

Trim off the ends of the zucchini, split them lengthwise, and drop the halves into boiling salted water. Cook 5 minutes or until tender. Drain. Scrape out the soft center portion, making a boat of each half. Discard the removed pulp. Grate the carrot on the coarse blade of a grater. There should be about ¾ cup.

Melt the 2 tablespoons butter in a saucepan and add the flour and curry powder, stirring. Add the fennel. Add the milk, stirring rapidly. When blended and smooth, add salt, pepper, grated carrot, and chopped pepper. Cook about 5 minutes.

Arrange the zucchini boats in a buttered baking dish and spoon the creamed carrot mixture into them. Combine the bread crumbs and cheese and sprinkle over the top. Dust with paprika, and dot with butter if you wish. Place under heated broiler and broil until golden brown and bubbling on top.   *Serves 4.*

○ *Golden Zucchini Tea Cake*

3½ cups flour, sifted	1 teaspoon vanilla extract
¾ teaspoon baking powder	4 large eggs
1½ teaspoons baking soda	2 cups grated unpeeled golden
1½ teaspoons salt	zucchini (½ golden and ½ green
2 teaspoons freshly grated lemon	may be used)
peel	1 cup chopped almonds or other
2 cups sugar	nuts
1 cup peanut or corn oil	1 cup golden raisins, rinsed,
	drained, and cut up

Mix together flour, baking powder, baking soda, salt, and lemon peel.

In a large mixing bowl beat together the sugar, oil, and vanilla until thoroughly combined. Beat in the eggs one at a time. Stir in the flour mixture alternately with the zucchini in several additions. Stir in the nuts and raisins.

Turn into greased loaf pans. I use 6 small pans that measure 5¾x3¼x2¼ inches. Or you can use three 8½x2½x3-inch pans. They should be half full.

Bake in a preheated 350° oven until a cake tester inserted in the center comes out clean—about 45 minutes for small loaves, 55–60 minutes for large loaves. Loosen edges and turn out on wire racks. Cool completely.

Other Ideas for Summer Squash

○ Summer squash marries well with many herbs—oregano, basil, garlic, curry, chili powder—as well as flavorful seeds such as cumin. It also has an affinity for tomatoes, onions, and olive oil.

○ Steam zucchini slices until crisp-tender, plunge into cold water, drain thoroughly, and dress with a mustardy vinaigrette.

○ Shred summer squash and carrots, stir-fry just until tender, and toss with lemon juice or sour cream and chopped basil.

- Squash buds and blooms make an unusual edible garnish. Dip them in thin batter and deep-fry.
- Alternate slices of 3 green and 3 yellow squash in a casserole. Combine 3 eggs with ½ cup milk and herbs to taste and pour over squash. Sprinkle with grated Monterey Jack cheese and cracker crumbs and bake at 350° F. for 30 minutes.
- For a wonderful roasted flavor, halve small summer squash lengthwise, brush with oil and a little chili powder, and cook on the outdoor grill until browned and tender.
- Although sliced squash gets soggy when frozen, squash purée freezes well and can be used in a variety of casseroles and soups. Cook squash with garlic and onions, purée in blender, food processor, or food mill, then freeze.
- Make summer squash pickles with your favorite brine. Yellow and green squash slices make an attractive combination. Use zucchini to make relish, too, or add slices to mixed pickles.
- See recipes for Quick Summer Squash Dip, Chicken Broth and Zucchini, and Purée of Squash Soup.

For a busy or weekend gardener, Swiss chard is one of the most reliable vegetables to have: it does not require picking at a special time, it tolerates both heat and cold, and only one planting is needed. Chard is a summer and fall vegetable related to beets. The plant is a bunch of large, long, shiny green leaves which have a thick white midrib, except for rhubarb chard, which has a brilliant red midrib. The variety Perpetual, which is early, has smaller leaves and thinner green midribs, and I think has the best flavor. All chard is very prolific, so eight to ten plants are enough for a large family (any extra can be frozen). The leaves are cut off individually, and I always leave the outside leaves and the very youngest on the plants to keep them healthy and growing. Chard will stand a light frost, which sweetens its flavor.

The seeds are sown directly in the garden. I plant three seeds together in one group, then other groups of three seeds ten inches apart. After the young plants are two inches high, I select the strongest plant of each group and cut out the others. I know gardeners who plant a row and make use of most of the young plants when five or six inches tall, leaving only some to mature. The thinnings are delicious steamed over rapidly boiling water and turned over frequently. Season with butter and lemon juice.

Because chard wilts very quickly and turns brown wherever bruised or cut, I do not use it in salads. When you pick it, handle it carefully and use it immediately if possible (though it can be refrigerated for several days). Both the leafy part and the steams are eaten, either together or separately.

○ Creamed Chard

Wash and cut out the thicker portion of chard midribs and put the leaves in a pot of water as each is prepared to prevent them from turning brown. Drain off water when all the leaves are prepared. Pour boiling water over the chard until covered. Add a teaspoon of salt. Turn the leaves over so that they get in contact with the hot water quickly. Cook uncovered for about 10 minutes, stirring now and then, and taste for doneness. The flavor increases as chard cooks, but it loses color when cooked too long.

Drain well in a colander, then chop and drain again. Return to pot or heat-resistant serving dish. Stir in butter and cream or undiluted cream of mushroom soup—⅓ can to 2 cups chopped chard—heat, and serve.

Note: The stems of the chard may also be used to extend your volume. In this case, cut the stems across in 1-inch pieces and put them in boiling water for 15 minutes, then add the chard leaves.

◦ Boiled Chard Stems

Cut chard stems to length desired and cook in salted boiling water for 20 minutes. Drain and serve with a tasty sauce, such as hollandaise or herb-seasoned sour cream.

◦ Rhubarb Chard Fritters

I'll never forget the year the beautiful rhubarb chard plant was introduced. Garden writers were at Fordhook for lunch, and Mr. Burpee wanted them to see and taste rhubarb chard fritters. My ovens were full of corn puddings, and the top of the stove had others being kept warm in pans of hot water, so I had to revitalize a kerosene stove to cook the fritters. I served them right from the pans— quite a rush! These fritters make a good hot hors d'oeuvre.

8 stalks rhubarb chard	1 egg, slightly beaten
1 cup flour	2 tablespoons oil or melted butter
½ teaspoon salt	⅔ cup milk
⅛ teaspoon paprika	Oil for deep frying

Cut the green leaves off the chard stems and save for boiled greens (see following recipe). Cut stems in 3-inch lengths, wash, and dry. Mix flour, salt, paprika, egg, oil or butter, and milk. Dip pieces of stem in this batter, covering them well.

Fry in deep fat heated to 375° F. or until hot enough to brown a 1-inch cube of bread in 1 minute. Fritters should be cooked through and delicately brown in 3 minutes. Drain on brown paper in a warm oven. *Serves 6-7.*

○ *Boiled Rhubarb Chard Leaves and Stems*

To preserve the lovely color of rhubarb chard in the cooked vegetable is a problem, for chard, a cousin of the red beet, bleeds when cut. I've found a way to use the stems and stalks and keep the color.

This has a light, refreshing flavor. You may add a spice such as cloves or mace, but I prefer it without. Salt should not be added when chard is cooking—it draws the sap out.

Wash 6 chard leaves and stalks. Cut off the leafy part and set it aside. Cut the stems into pieces as long as will fit in your pot horizontally. Add 1 or 2 bay leaves, according to quantity. Pour boiling water, to which 1 teaspoon of white vinegar per cup of water has been added, over the stems until they are a little more than covered. Boil for 15 minutes uncovered. Then add the chopped leaves and cook, uncovered, for 15 minutes more. Drain and save the bright red water. Remove the bay leaves. Cut the stems into 1-inch lengths.

Make a sauce with 1 cup of the red liquor: dissolve 1½ teaspoons cornstarch in it, then add a scant ¼ teaspoon salt and 1 teaspoon sugar. Cook until color is clear and bright. Stir in 2 teaspoons butter until melted. Pour over the chard leaves and stems, and warm in an uncovered double boiler, heavy pan, or microwave oven. **Serves 2.**

Other Ideas for Chard

○ Basil, garlic, oregano, and nutmeg go well with chard.
○ Add several handfuls of diced chard leaves to cream of potato soup.
○ To stir-fry chard, first sauté a garlic clove in oil. Discard garlic, add cut-up chard leaves, and fry for 3 minutes. Stir in soy sauce and sliced water chestnuts and simmer 3 more minutes.
○ Use cooked chopped chard leaves in recipes calling for spinach (see ideas in discussion of spinach). Use stripped chard stems as you would asparagus or celery (see discussions of them).

- Add cooked chopped chard leaves and ribs to stuffing for turkey if you like moist stuffing.
- Make a layer of chard in a casserole of scalloped potatoes or turnips.
- In France, steamed chard is often served with a béchamel sauce and sausages—a tasty combination. Italians cook chard leaves with other greens—mild and pungent—to serve with pork.

It was not known in Asia or Europe until the Americas were discovered, yet I doubt that any vegetable has made a tastier impact on foods than the tomato. Tomatoes are native to a hot climate, and because it takes up to four months from germination to get a ripe tomato from most varieties, tomato seeds must be started indoors in many areas. Sow them six to eight weeks before the last frosts are expected.

There are tomatoes of many types and sizes, and so many varieties that the choice can be bewildering. I recommend that you choose those that have been bred for disease resistance. The value of the hybrids and disease-resistant tomatoes is very apparent in your own garden when you plant some older varieties along with them.

Nevertheless, my own favorite variety is neither a hybrid nor particularly disease-resistant. It is a large, flavorful tomato called Burpee's Delicious. The largest tomato ever grown was a Burpee's Delicious that weighed 6½ pounds. If you are trying to get a big tomato for a harvest show, you might try this one.

Small yellow tomatoes have been in existence for years. They make an exceptionally lovely marmalade and are nice spiced as a conserve. I think they are less acid than small cherry tomatoes, and they don't squirt as much when bitten into.

Burpee's Jubilee was introduced the year of the golden jubilee of King George and Queen Mary of England. It is a large, beautiful golden-orange fruit with a flavor and texture different from red tomatoes. It tastes much sweeter, although I understand its sugar content is no greater than reds. I always plant a few Jubilee plants because there are times when I just don't want that red tomato color on the dish. Jubilee has a firm, pleasant texture. It makes a beautiful yellow juice and attractive aspic and jam.

If you would like to use your canned tomatoes in a winter salad, try Roma. Roma is a very firm tomato with thicker flesh, fewer seeds, and less water than most other varieties. It is known as a paste-type tomato and is good for sauces. The plum-shaped fruit is also easy to pack into jars.

Burpee's Long-Keeper tomato is just that—a much better keeper than other garden tomatoes gathered at the end of the season. Although the skin does not get bright red, the flavor is preferable to other stored green tomatoes and most that you find in grocery stores in winter.

No matter what varieties you choose, set your plants deep in the soil when transplanting. It doesn't hurt the plant to have some of the stem buried. Try to get some well-rotted horse manure to put around the growing plants. I am an advocate of pruning tomato plants and prefer staking them to growing them in wire towers. It is harder to prune plants growing in towers, and if not pruned the tomatoes will ripen later and the crop will be smaller. (But I must admit towers are handier to use.) Prune out the young auxillary branches that grow where the leaf joins the stem.

I have found it to be true that planting marigolds, especially the tall American types (not the odorless varieties), will reduce the appearance of the horned tomato caterpillar. If you see just the stems of the leaves and a lot of black droppings, look for this creature, who looks like he came from outer space. He is at least as large as your thumb.

If you have tried without much success to grow tomatoes on the windowsill or in a greenhouse in winter, a lack of pollination could be the cause. To aid pollination indoors, tap the blossoms so that pollen drops from stamens to pistils. Your fruit will develop better. The small, early-bearing tomatoes, like Burpee's Pixie hybrid, are favored for growing in pots.

Please let your tomatoes ripen on the vine so they will be sweeter and more nutritious. They will also peel more easily. However, the day comes when the gardener hears that the temperature will drop to the low thirties. This is the time to pick all but a few of the fruits left on the vines (the ones left just might not get frostbitten, especially if you throw a blanket over them). Fruits showing some color will ripen on a sunny windowsill, so separate them from the green ones.

Wash and dry the green tomatoes and those that are starting to look yellow green. Discard any with bruises or blemishes or cracks, or make mincemeat or relish with them. Get a carton and a pile of newspapers. Crinkle some paper in the bottom of the box, then wrap each tomato separately with half a newspaper sheet. Start with the greenest ones so they will be at the bottom, and proceed to fill the box, but do not pack it tightly. Store where the temperature is fairly constantly at 55°–60° F. The tomatoes start ripening in about three weeks. Watch for any dampness and remove the rotting tomatoes. I have kept tomatoes until mid-November.

I prefer raw tomatoes to cooked. I frequently serve a platter of sliced tomatoes with snipped parsley and/or chives and a dab of cottage cheese on each slice. Let each person add salt and pepper to taste. If your family likes raw onion, a thin slice placed on the tomato is nice, too.

°Stewed Tomatoes

In preparing tomatoes for stewing, dip in boiling water and then the skin will pull off easily. Cut them across the center and press gently so that most of the seeds come out (discard seeds). Put tomatoes in any pot that is not aluminum or iron and let them sit for about 10 minutes, until some juice covers the bottom. Add 4 fresh basil leaves to a quart of raw tomatoes (chopped celery and onion may also be added) and let simmer, stirring frequently, until cooked down to about a pint and a half. Season with ½ teaspoon salt and 1 teaspoon sugar per pint of tomatoes.

Stewed tomatoes may be thickened with 1 teaspoon seasoned bread crumbs to 1 pint cooked tomatoes, added just before serving. Or add 1½ teaspoons cornstarch or fine tapioca to some cold tomato juice in a cup and mix well. Then add to hot tomatoes, stir it in, and let cook with the tomatoes, stirring frequently. Thickening with flour spoils the color.

°Tomato Pudding

A nice change and surprise is to use your own golden tomato purée with golden raisins in this recipe.

4 slices white bread, toasted and cut into small cubes	2 tablespoons raisins, pressed down
4 cups thick tomato juice or purée	¼ teaspoon allspice
½ teaspoon dried basil	Salt (if tomato juice or purée is not salted)
3 tablespoons brown sugar	1 tablespoon butter

Put half the toast cubes in the bottom of a buttered baking dish. Heat together all the other ingredients except butter and pour over the toast cubes. Place remaining toast cubes on top and press down a little. Dot with butter and bake at 325° F. for 30 minutes or until heated through. *Serves 4-5.*

°Fried Tomatoes

This is an excellent side dish to serve with liver and bacon. Use firm, almost ripe tomatoes. Do not peel. Slice tomatoes ½ inch thick. Mix equal parts seasoned bread crumbs and flour on a flat plate and use to coat tomato slices on both sides. Salt the slices.

Cover the bottom of a fry pan with oil and heat. Put tomatoes in pan in one layer. Shake a little sugar over the slices. Turn them when slightly browned, brown second side, then put on flat heated platter. Pour a little milk into the fry pan and stir in what is stuck to the pan to make a gravy. Pour gravy over the tomatoes.

°Stir-Fried Green Tomatoes and Peppers

Serve some form of rice with the meal when using this as the vegetable. Serve with fish or beef.

2 tablespoons vegetable oil
¾ cup green peppers peeled and cut into strips
¾ cup red sweet peppers peeled and cut into strips
1 cup sliced mushrooms
1 cup celery cut into ½-inch slices, strings removed
2 tablespoons chopped onion
½ clove garlic, crushed

1 teaspoon chopped fresh oregano or ¼ teaspoon dried
¼ teaspoon celery salt (ordinary salt will do)
½ teaspoon chopped fresh hot red pepper, or a grinding of black pepper
4 hard green tomatoes (about 2 inches in diameter), cut into wedges
2 tablespoons teriyaki sauce, or ¼ teaspoon sugar, ¼ teaspoon salt, and ½ teaspoon wine vinegar

Heat the oil in a skillet or wok and add everything but the tomatoes and sauce. Stir-fry over medium-high heat until peppers are crisp-tender. Remove the garlic, add the tomatoes and sauce and cook only until heated through. *Serves 3-4.*

° Whole Tomato Aspic

Prepare at least four hours before serving. If you are going to serve the aspic on a bed of lettuce and not in a mixed salad, add ½ cup each finely chopped carrot and celery to the hot tomatoes.

2 cups canned tomatoes	**1 teaspoon sugar**
1 envelope unflavored gelatin	**½ teaspoon Worcestershire sauce**
	or 4 basil leaves, crushed

Put 1 cup tomatoes in a 7x3-inch loaf pan and sprinkle gelatin over them. Heat the rest of the tomatoes with sugar and Worcestershire or basil and bring just to a boil. Remove basil leaves, if used. Add the hot tomato to the loaf pan and stir until well mixed. Let cool, uncovered, then stir and refrigerate to firm.

Variation: For an attractive Christmas appetizer or buffet platter, make aspic in a shallow pan. When firm, cut it into star shapes and top with a cream-cheese ball studded with a green olive. Serve on a bed of bright green lettuce or spinach.

° Tomato Aspic and Lettuce

This is one of our favorite cold-weather salads. Instead of using tasteless winter tomatoes I substitute an aspic made from my own canned tomatoes. I cut the aspic into cubes and mix it with torn lettuce in a 12-inch bowl, then add ½ cup cut-up young celery leaves, and ¼ cup each chopped onion and fresh parsley. I use French's Old-Fashioned French Dressing using leftover pickle juice in place of water and a combination of olive and vegetable oils.

Serves 4-6.

Other Ideas for Tomatoes

° Basil is the classic tomato herb. Dill, oregano, thyme, parsley, and chili powder also go well with tomatoes.

○ Stuff cherry or plum tomatoes with cream cheese flavored with fresh basil, watercress, or minced radishes. Or try a guacamole or curried tuna stuffing.

○ For a simple but beautiful salad, arrange slices of red and yellow tomatoes and sprinkle with lemon juice, oil, and a generous amount of chopped fresh dill.

○ Marinate cherry tomatoes and small fresh white mushrooms in oil, vinegar, garlic, oregano, and basil overnight. Chill to serve as an appetizer, or heat over high flame, stirring, just until heated through for a side dish.

○ Make tabbouleh by soaking fine bulgur (cracked wheat) until fluffy. Squeeze out water and add chopped seeded tomatoes, scallions, mint, parsley, olive oil, and lemon juice.

○ For Spanish rice, purée 1½ cups peeled, seeded, chopped tomatoes. Sauté chopped onions and garlic in ¼ cup oil until soft, stir in 2 cups rice and tomato purée, and simmer covered over low heat until rice is tender.

○ Peel and halve tomatoes, top with mayonnaise, minced scallions, then grated Cheddar, and bake at 325° F. for 20 minutes.

○ Pipérade, a French sauce, is delicious with omelets or scrambled eggs. To make it, sauté thin strips of green pepper, sliced onion, garlic, and chopped tomatoes in olive oil until thickened. If you like, stir in thin strips of smoky ham.

○ Green tomatoes can be used in many ways: you can pickle green cherry tomatoes or sliced large green tomatoes, grind them to make relish, or make tomato chutney with chopped tomatoes, peppers, apples, raisins, brown sugar, vinegar, and spices of your choice.

○ Add some thick tomato pulp to a plain soufflé mixture for a delicate color and flavor. A little tomato purée is also good in Welsh rabbit.

○ Try a fresh tomato pizza: overlap very ripe tomato slices to cover a partially baked pizza crust. Sprinkle with olive oil and chopped fresh basil, oregano, and parsley, and add a generous topping of mozzarella cheese. Heat at 400° F. until mozzarella is lightly browned.

○ See recipe for Green Tomato Pie. See also Hot Tomato Juice; Carrot and Tomato Broth.

PARKER LEIGHTON

7
Fall and Winter Vegetables

As the gardening season draws to an end, I get a renewed interest in my garden plot and try to expand its life beyond the first few frosts.

Most of the vegetables in the fall garden are those that require a long growing season, like leeks and parsnips, or those that mature in the cooler, shortening days of fall, such as cauliflower.

The seeds of fall root crops are sown in the garden by the end of June; those of nonheading green vegetables, such as kale and escarole, I sow in early July. Heading vegetables, such as cabbage, Chinese cabbage, and cauliflower, are best started in a seed bed or indoors in late June.

When night temperatures cool down, I can once again plant some of the early garden vegetables, including the butterhead types of lettuce, and with luck I get a second crop of peas. A second crop of kohlrabi is sweetened by a frosty night. And it is good to be able to enjoy the celery, which I have fed and watered religiously from July on.

There is one big advantage in planning for a fall garden: the absence of those awful black flea beetles that devour seedlings growing in June. But the cabbage butterfly has laid its eggs on all members of the cabbage family, and I must keep an eye out for the hatching green worms. I make a habit of shaking rotenone on all those plants regularly after each rain. (Insects seem to know which are the most tender and flavorful leaves. I have come to the conclusion that a test for the best plant foods would be to observe those which insects prefer.)

West Central Europe is the origin of this member of the cabbage family, as its name suggests. But it is in England and not Belgium that Brussels sprouts are most popular.

It takes a long time for Brussels sprouts to form their little heads, about four and a half months from planting seeds, but fortunately frost does not hurt them. The sprouts develop along the stem, well protected by leaves. When people see sprouts growing for the first time they are often surprised, since the seed-catalog pictures show only some of the plant, with the leaves on the stem removed.

Seeds may be planted in a seed bed in the garden in late May or early June for transplanting later. The plants are big and must be set at least two feet apart. Work some fertilizer into the soil, and add some lime if your soil is acid. It is best not to plant sprouts where other members of the cabbage family have recently grown.

Fortunate indeed is the gardener who can keep aphids off Brussels sprouts. Treating them with a diluted detergent sometimes helps. Do not be in a hurry to use sprouts, for as the weather gets colder they have a better flavor—I have even picked them when snow was on the ground—but you should harvest while the heads are still firm, bright green, and one to two inches in diameter. You need a sharp serrated knife to cut them off the stem. Leaves should be stripped off the stem as the sprouts develop from the bottom upward, but leave the top tuft of leaves untouched for a prolonged harvest. Put any frozen sprouts in cold water immediately to thaw.

For best flavor, cook sprouts immediately after harvesting,

though they will keep a few days in the refrigerator. Many sprout haters have experienced only stale, cabbagy old sprouts and don't realize that small fresh ones have a refined, even delicate flavor.

To cook, cut an X in the bottom of larger sprouts to make cooking even. Pour boiling water over sprouts to a level of two inches and cook seven to twelve minutes, or until heads are barely tender when pierced with a fork. The important thing in serving sprouts is to get the cooking water out of them and have them still hot. I advise letting them drain in a strainer over hot water.

○ Sautéed Sprouts with Ginger

1 pint Brussels sprouts	⅛ teaspoon salt
6 slices fresh ginger	⅛ teaspoon ground cumin
¼ cup vegetable oil	1 egg beaten with 1 tablespoon
¼ cup whole-wheat flour	water

Clean the sprouts and blanch in boiling water for 5 minutes. Drain well. Simmer the ginger in the oil in a fry pan or wok for 10 minutes. Mix the flour, salt, and cumin in a small paper bag. Dip the sprouts in the egg mixture and shake them in the flour mixture. Sauté them in the ginger-flavored oil for 10 minutes.   *Serves 4.*

Other Ideas for Brussels Sprouts

○ Good seasonings for sprouts include garlic, dill, ginger, nutmeg, or cloves added to a white sauce.

○ Small boiled and marinated sprouts are good for a cocktail snack. Serve with toothpicks in them.

○ Simmer sprouts and chopped celery until tender, then fold into a cheese sauce.

○ For a traditional French holiday dish, mix cooked sprouts with cooked chestnuts and butter. Or use almonds and sour cream.

○ Braise sprouts, onions, and mushrooms in bacon fat. Top with grated Cheddar and crumbled bacon.

○ Cook sprouts until barely tender, roll in seasoned flour, then

beaten egg, then fine bread crumbs, and fry in deep fat until golden brown.
- Moisten cooked sprouts with a curried cream sauce and serve in a rice ring.

Have you ever noticed how beautiful a cabbage plant is right after a rain, with droplets of silvery water sparkling all over its leaves? A young plant looks like a large green rose. It is no wonder that ornamental cabbages have been developed for use in flower beds.

Cabbage is an ancient vegetable. It has been grown for at least four thousand years. In its wild form it is found along the chalk coasts of England, Denmark, and Central Europe, where it is a biennial that produces seeds the second year of growth. Early cabbages all had loose green heads and contained more vitamins than the naturally blanched tight heads of today.

Cabbage seeds for a fall crop are planted in early June in a seed bed outdoors or inside. They do not require a lot of water for germination. Seedlings growing in wet soil will be susceptible to fungus root diseases. Further precautions to prevent this are to select disease-resistant varieties, plant treated seeds, and never plant cabbage in the same place in successive years.

When large enough to handle, set the young cabbage plants eighteen to twenty inches apart in a row and water with Transplantone. The appearance of cabbage suggests that it needs above-average water and food to produce a nice large head. Apply high-nitrogen fertilizer two weeks after planting. While the heads are not yet formed, the white cabbage butterfly loves to lay her eggs in them and lots of tiny green worms hatch. Look for them before they get larger and have a more voracious appetite. Holes in the leaves, eaten edges, or black spots are telltale signs that the worms are there. I dust regularly with rotenone. The head develops from within so the dust does not get into the edible part.

Cabbage heads will split after heavy rains. Should your heads get nice and big but you wish to leave them in the garden for a few more weeks, give the plants a twist to break a few roots and keep them from absorbing as much water as they normally do.

Early cabbage is discussed under summer vegetables (see also Chinese cabbage, discussed later). The varieties of heading cabbage to select for your late garden are those listed in catalogs as fall or winter cabbage. The three distinctive types are those that produce tight heads whose leaves are smooth and have thick ribs, the looser heads of crinkled darker green leaves of the Savoy and the magnificent red cabbages. I suggest growing a few of each type, as they have distinctive uses: the harder heads for slaw, sauerkraut, and winter storage, the Savoy for green boiled cabbage, and the reds primarily for their color—but I think their flavor is different too. I have noticed that the reds will tolerate colder weather than the green ones. Their texture is also a bit tougher, so they require longer cooking or marinating. A little vinegar or lemon juice in the cooking water will preserve the red color.

The most common way to cook cabbage is simply to cut it up and boil it. It may be shredded or cut in wedges and cooked in water or steamed until tender but still a bit crispy. When boiling whole cabbage, make a few cuts deep into the head so that water can penetrate. Place whole head in a serving dish, cut it almost through in wedges so it will open up, and pour a nicely flavored sauce over it. Use cheese, cumin, ginger, or celery in the sauce and sprinkle paprika over the top.

∘Corned Beef and Cabbage

I think there is nothing better on a cold winter day than corned beef and cabbage. Follow the instructions on the corned-beef package. Three-quarters of an hour before the meat is fully cooked add wedges of cabbage, carrots, and onions to the pot and raise the heat on the burner so the liquid will return to a boil. I like to add a bay leaf or two, a few peppercorns, and cut-up celery leaves.

○ *Sweet-and-Sour Cabbage*

4 cups (not packed) shredded red cabbage	2 rounded tablespoons brown sugar
3 tablespoons white vinegar	¼ teaspoon ground ginger
½ teaspoon salt	¼ teaspoon allspice
1 tablespoon cornstarch	2 tablespoons butter or margarine

Put cabbage in a pot with boiling water just to cover. Add 1 table-spoon of the vinegar and the salt. When cooked but still a bit crisp, remove from heat and drain well. Save 1 cup of the liquor for sauce. Keep cabbage warm over steam while making the sauce.

Dissolve cornstarch in the cup of reserved liquor. Add remaining ingredients and cook over low heat until clear and thickened, stirring constantly. Pour over the cabbage in an ovenproof serving dish. Mix well and keep warm in oven until ready to serve. (This is a cooked dish that freezes well—just put it in a plastic container with a tight lid and freeze.)   *Serves 6.*

Other Ideas for Cabbage

- ○ Coleslaw can be seasoned with almost any fresh summer herb.
- ○ In cooked cabbage try dill, celery seed, cayenne or black pepper, ginger, or allspice.
- ○ Season boiled or steamed shredded cabbage with sour cream and dill or fennel leaves.
- ○ Coleslaw is usually made with a creamy dressing, but I like it best with a refreshing oil, vinegar, and herb dressing. For color I add shredded carrot and chopped cucumber pickle and lots of fresh parsley. You can also add chopped green pepper, celery, onion, crumbled bacon, or pineapple.
- ○ Cook corned beef with cabbage for hearty winter fare, but in summer make a salad of corned beef cubes, raw shredded cabbage, and potatoes, with a mustardy mayonnaise dressing.

- Parboil large cabbage leaves for 8 minutes, cut midribs out, roll leaves around a ground-meat stuffing, and simmer in tomato sauce for 1½ hours.
- Make cream of cabbage soup, adding sour cream after shredded cabbage has cooked tender. Top with grated cheese.
- Use parboiled large cabbage leaves to line a loaf pan. Add shredded cabbage to your favorite meat loaf mixture and fill the pan. When baked, unmold and serve with a spicy tomato sauce.
- To make colcannon, mash hot potatoes and leeks, then beat in cooked shredded cabbage. (Any leftovers make delicious patties fried in bacon fat.)
- Don't discard the hard cores and stumps of cabbage from your garden: peel off any woody skin, slice into rounds, and simmer until tender—good with dill and garlic butter.
- See recipe for stir-fried cabbage. Cabbage may be used in borscht, see index.

I think of cauliflower as an aristocrat among vegetables. It is beautiful but temperamental: it has to be protected from the sun to keep a nice white head, it will not head properly if it gets too hot, and it will not withstand frost. Furthermore, it is not suitable for a small garden, as the plants need such a lot of room and are harvested only once.

Some varieties of cauliflower take only three months to produce nice heads, but they develop best in cool weather, so it is a fall garden crop. Seeds are sown in early July in a seed bed or flat, and when seedlings are five weeks old they are planted in the garden two feet apart. Set the plants deep in the soil up to the base of the first true leaves. Birds do not seem to be as interested in plants set out in midsummer as they are in the May and June transplants. I strongly advise the use of Transplantone when setting out plants, especially in the summer, as it promotes good root growth.

It used to be that cauliflower leaves had to be drawn together and tied over the developing head to keep it white, but now there are varieties with leaves that grow curving over the head. But do peek under the leaves now and then to be sure the cabbage worms are not feasting on the young head. Use rotenone or Sevin to kill them.

Cauliflower heads stay in good shape longer than broccoli heads, but the florets will separate and grow tall, especially after some warm days, so I advise harvesting the cauliflower crop as soon as it is ready rather than leaving the heads on the plants. They keep well in a ventilated plastic bag for up to five days in the refrigerator and also freeze well.

My favorite of the cauliflowers is the Purple Head variety. I had overlooked it in the catalog, but one year when walking through the vegetable trials in September, I was struck by its beauty and brought a head in to use as a centerpiece on the table. I do not know why purple cauliflower is not grown commercially—it is not a new vegetable and is listed in old seed catalogs as green cauliflower. I presume that it is considered lowlier than the pampered white head.

It does take longer for purple cauliflower to form a head (I have wondered some years if it ever would). But finally, sometimes even after the first frost, the head forms and grows quickly. It has better color when the sunshine gets on it, so don't tie up its leaves. The purple color is in the sap, and it disappears in cooking—the cauliflower becomes a lovely green resembling broccoli, but it has a firmer head and a more delicate flavor that is so good only butter should be used with it. It is excellent for freezing.

I like white cauliflower best eaten raw as finger food or in salads, but you can boil it, stir-fry it in oil, or steam it (whole cauliflower takes 20–30 minutes, florets about 10 minutes).

○ Boiled Cauliflower

The usual way to serve cauliflower is to cut up the head, boil it 10–15 minutes, and serve it with a cream sauce. I advise draining it well over steam for a few minutes before serving in order to get all the water out.

A more glamorous way to serve cauliflower is to cook the head whole. Use your spaghetti cooker or blancher. Put the cauliflower stem end down, pour boiling water over it, and boil for 30 minutes or less according to size of head. (A little lemon juice, milk, or sugar in the cooking water helps keep cauliflower white.) A cauliflower head cooks faster if you hollow out the stem with a paring knife. Drain cauliflower well, then pour sauce over it—lemon butter, cheese sauce, or hollandaise. A bit of color, such as finely chopped parsley or red peppers, is a nice touch. Or you can sprinkle grated cheese on top and place the cauliflower under a broiler for a minute or two until it is lightly browned.

○ Fried Cauliflower

Dip small cauliflower florets in a beaten mixture of 1 egg and 1 tablespoon water. Roll in mixture of ½ cup whole-wheat or white flour, ½ teaspoon salt, and ½ teaspoon cumin seed. Heat a few slices of fresh ginger in oil until fragrant, then remove. Stir-fry cauliflower in ginger-flavored oil and drain on brown paper. Cooked this way, it is very good served with beef. Or stir-fry it with sliced scallions and slivered ham and serve with brown rice.

Other Ideas for Cauliflower

○ Flavor cauliflower with thyme, basil, garlic, chives, lemon juice, or ginger.

- For cauliflower appetizers, serve florets either raw or steamed until tender-crisp, then chilled. Use both white and purple cauliflower for contrast, and serve with dips: guacamole, curried mayonnaise, Russian dressing.
- Steam cauliflower just until tender, then toss with sour cream, a drop of Tabasco, and plenty of snipped chives and parsley or dill.
- For creamy rich cauliflower soup, cook florets until tender in lemon- or tarragon-flavored chicken broth. Purée in blender with a little milk, then stir in cream. Serve hot, sprinkled with nutmeg, or cold, decorated with lemon slices or shredded carrot.
- Cook a whole head of cauliflower, then "frost" it with a mixture of mayonnaise, mustard, and grated cheese. Bake until cheese melts.
- Dip cauliflower florets in batter, deep-fry, and sprinkle with grated cheese.
- Mash and whip very tender cooked cauliflower as you would potatoes, adding butter, milk, grated cheese, and an egg. Sprinkle with bread crumbs, dot with butter, and bake at 350° F. for 20 minutes.
- Cook cauliflower leaves with mixed greens.
- Cauliflower can be substituted for broccoli or used with it in many recipes—see discussion of broccoli for ideas.
- Add cauliflower pieces (including peeled stems) to mixed pickles.

This celery-flavored root vegetable is better known in Europe than in America, perhaps because it grows best in cool weather. But, since it is a slow grower, it has to be started in May for a September crop. It took me a long time to find out how to grow good celeriac bulbs (which are also known as celery knobs, celery roots, or turnip-rooted celery). Mine were small and fibrous until I learned that to promote more top growth to the bulb and fewer side roots, celeriac seedlings should be planted in a mounded row, and as the bulb develops the earth should be pushed away from the crown gradually. Celeriac needs a lot of food and water, but bugs leave it alone.

When you pull celeriac, cut the small roots off in the garden and hose it off outside. Save the younger leaves for seasoning. The surface is so irregular I suggest using a scrubbing brush to clean it. The top is more tender than the base, which sometimes is pithy when the plants have not grown well.

Celeriac is used primarily in soups and stews. I like it as a substitute for potato. If you are going to cook celeriac, it is easier to peel after it has been boiled. It cooks faster than potatoes—diced and boiled, it will be tender in about ten minutes. A little lemon juice in the cooking water will help keep it white. Like celery, it may also be braised in broth.

Celeriac is also peeled and added raw to salads. Because it darkens when exposed to air, peeled raw celeriac should be kept in acidulated or salty water until ready to use.

°Creamed Celeriac

Scrub and boil whole celeriac in lightly salted water for 20 minutes. Peel and cut into cubes. Prepare Basic White Sauce (page 30), 1 cup sauce for 2 cups diced celeriac. Add 1 tablespoon cut-up young celery leaves to each cup of sauce. Mix celeriac and sauce at least 5 minutes before serving. Sprinkle some paprika on top.

°Celeriac Salad

4 celeriac roots
Salt
1⅓ cups oil
⅔ cup vinegar
½ teaspoon chopped parsley or
basil
Paprika to taste
¼ teaspoon celery seed

¾-1 cup diced celery
¼ cup chopped onion or ⅓ cup
snipped chives
⅓ cup chopped fresh mint
¼ cup chopped sweet red pepper
¼ cup grated carrot
2 tablespoons mayonnaise
Lettuce

Clean celeriac, boil for 20 minutes, peel, and cube. Mix in some salt. Combine oil, vinegar, salad herbs, paprika, and celery seed. Pour half this dressing over celeriac while it is still warm.

Combine celery, onion or chives, mint, red pepper, carrot, and mayonnaise, and add to celeriac. Add as much of the remaining oil-and-vinegar dressing as you think the salad needs. Mix all together and serve on lettuce. This can be served warm, or it can be made a day or several hours ahead and served cold. *Serves 4*

Other Ideas for Celeriac

° Celeriac's flavor is complemented by basil, parsley, tarragon, chervil, lemon juice, and mustard.
° Cut celeriac into julienne strips and immediately toss in vinaigrette. Chill and serve mounded on lettuce leaves. Add grated carrot or beets for color.
° Grate celeriac into coleslaw.
° For Danish celeriac salad, shred celeriac into acidulated water,

then squeeze dry and add whipped cream, mayonnaise, mustard, and chopped parsley.

◦ Rumanians cook celeriac for salad, slice it, add oil, vinegar, and parsley, and garnish with sour pickles and black olives. Some chopped ham is a good addition.

◦ Celeriac is delicious sautéed: melt butter in a heavy pan with a lid, add peeled celeriac sliced ¼ inch thick, cover, and cook, shaking now and then, until slices are tender and delicately brown.

◦ Pass well-cooked celeriac through a ricer, and beat with butter until light—good with rich-flavored roasts.

◦ Slice celeriac into rounds 1 inch thick. Blanch 5 minutes, then scoop a hollow ½ inch deep in each slice. Combine the diced scooped-out pulp with sautéed diced carrots, mushrooms, and onions, fill each hollow and make a mound, sprinkle with grated Parmesan cheese, and bake at 350° F. until cheese is lightly browned.

◦ Leftover creamed celeriac is excellent for thickening soups— use a blender and some soup stock to smooth it out.

◦ Many recipes using celery or potatoes can be adapted to celeriac—see ideas where those vegetables are discussed (especially Potato Salad).

I always have celery in my refrigerator to use for flavoring as well as a vegetable on its own, and I look forward to the season when I can cut it from the garden. It really is a treat to have home-grown celery; it has so much more flavor than the commercial stalks. But it takes a long time, at least six months from seed sowing to cutting size, and a lot of high-nitrogen fertilizer, the kind used on lawns, for it is the vegetative part of the plant that is eaten. I do not recommend growing celery unless you have a large vegetable garden with easy access to water. It will not grow well in a hot, dry climate.

The home gardener should grow the green Pascal or the self-blanching type of celery. My favorite is Burpee's Fordhook, which antedated the Pascal types but like them has tender green stalks. Remember, green celery contains more vitamins and flavor than blanched celery.

Celery seeds are used for seasoning, especially pickles and salad dressing. These are produced the second year of the plant's growth and only where winters are warm.

If you have a springhouse or a cool earth-floor cellar as some old houses do, you can dig up celery plants and store them upright in a crate for a few months. They will need watering now and then.

Celery seed is sown ten weeks before the last frost in your area. The young plants are slow-growing; they take at least two and a half months to reach the proper size for transplanting. Celery is the only vegetable garden plant I know of that can be given too much room—it will spread out like a bush rather than grow tall and compact. When I set mine out I plant two rows ten inches apart and place the plants in the rows five inches apart so that they zigzag across the two rows. When I apply extra fertilizer every six weeks I put it on the soil between the two rows. I hate to fertilize weeds, so I always put it only where I want it.

Fortunately, celery is not bothered by bugs, but late in the season you may find a yellow, black, or green caterpillar on it—just pick it off.

Celery is sensitive to frost, so if an early frost is predicted do protect it. Often there is an early frost and then a month of glorious weather during which you can enjoy your own flavorful celery.

Always leave some of the root on a bunch when you bring it in from the garden. There is a nice tender heart in it.

Nobody likes to eat celery strings. To really enjoy celery, you should remove the strings—the plant's food pipeline—from the stalks to make it more tender and palatable. To string celery, hold a stalk, leaves up, in your left hand, with outside of stalk toward the right. Grasp the top of the stalk by placing your right hand around it thumb down and pull the top of the stalk back over your hand. The stalk will snap below your thumb and you will see the strings connecting the two pieces. Pull down gently to the bottom of the stalk, and you will have all the strings, about eight, in your right hand. If you have pulled out only a few strings, break the stalk in half in the same manner and pull the remaining strings down each half.

∘Celery in Cheese Sauce

You may use other seasonings instead of cheese in the sauce, such as ¼ teaspoon curry powder or ½ teaspoon cumin or caraway seeds. Taste until you get the flavor you like. I like this dish best with fish.

2 cups celery (strings removed) cut into ½-inch pieces
2 sprigs fresh tarragon or oregano
1 tablespoon butter
1½ tablespoons flour
1 cup milk
⅓ cup grated mild Cheddar cheese
1 firm medium-size tomato, skinned, seeded, and cut in teaspoon-size pieces
Seasoned bread crumbs
Grated Parmesan cheese

Cook celery and tarragon or oregano together in just enough water to cover until tender. Drain well. Remove herb sprigs.

Melt the butter, add the flour, and stir until bubbly. Add the milk and cheese and stir until smooth.

Mix the cheese sauce, celery, and tomato. Put in a baking dish. Sprinkle with bread crumbs and a little Parmesan cheese. Heat in a 325° oven and brown under the broiler before serving.   *Serves 4.*

∘Sweet-and-Sour Celery

3 cups sliced celery (strings removed)
1 egg, beaten
2 tablespoons flour
2 tablespoons sugar
¾ teaspoon salt
⅛ teaspoon pepper or 1 teaspoon diced fresh hot red pepper
2 tablespoons vinegar
1 cup water
¼ cup sour cream or plain yogurt

Cook the celery in briskly boiling lightly salted water until tender. Drain and keep hot.

Blend together egg, flour, sugar, salt, and pepper in a saucepan. Blend in the vinegar and water. Cook over medium heat, stirring constantly, until mixture comes to a boil. Remove from heat and add sour cream or yogurt. Add celery. *Serves 6*

°*Celery Shrimp Kowloon*

When cold weather threatens, I quickly make use of the frost-sensitive celery in the garden. In the past, when I protected it by piling leaves over it, the field mice found it to be a well-stocked winter resort and ate out all the hearts. I found Alex Hawkes's recipe for celery shrimp and have made my own adaptation, using what I have available where appropriate. Serve this dish with soy sauce and rice.

6 cups celery (strings removed) cut diagonally into ¾-inch slices
4 tablespoons butter
¾ cup seasoned bread cubes
5-ounce can drained water chestnuts, thinly sliced, or 1 cup sliced raw Jerusalem artichokes

1 can condensed cream of chicken or cream of shrimp soup
2 peeled and chopped fresh pimentos
3 cups diced cooked shrimp

Cook the celery in briskly boiling lightly salted water until raw taste has gone but celery is still crisp. Drain and cool under cold running water to stop the cooking process. Drain again.

In a fry pan, melt the butter and lightly brown the bread cubes. Put half the cubes aside, mix the rest with everything else, including celery, and spread mixture in a shallow casserole. Sprinkle the remaining bread cubes on top. Be sure you add any butter from the fry pan. Bake at 350° F. for 30 minutes. *Serves 5-6*

° Braised Celery

This is a dish to prepare when celery is plentiful.

Remove coarse outer celery stalks and save for seasoning soups. Cut the heart in half lengthwise. It will hold together when you have left some of the root on the bunch. Place the celery in a baking dish, cover with meat stock, and bake at 400° F. for 25 minutes or until tender. Or braise celery in a fry pan covered with a spatter lid for 25 minutes, until almost all the liquid has cooked away.

° Celery and Apple Salad

This is most attractive served on individual plates in a nest of small Boston lettuce leaves or other head lettuce in pieces small enough so they are convenient to eat.

Drain an 11-ounce can of mandarin orange sections and put juice in a mixing bowl. Add ¼ cup golden or dark raisins to the juice. String and dice enough celery to make 1½ cups. Mix the celery, orange sections, raisins, and juice with 2 tablespoons mayonnaise. Pare and dice 3 medium-size Golden Delicious or McIntosh apples and immediately fold them into the mixture. Spoon the salad onto lettuce. Cut-up dried figs may be substituted for the raisins, and nuts may be added. *Serves 4-5.*

Other Ideas for Celery

- ° Peanut butter and cream cheese contrast agreeably with the texture, taste, and color of raw celery, and stuffed celery makes a healthful snack or appetizer.
- ° Make celery curls for garnish by cutting celery into 4-inch lengths, then slitting each piece into narrow lengthwise slices, leaving ½-inch base. Drop pieces in ice water to curl.
- ° To make pretty celery pinwheels, mix Roquefort and cream cheese, fill hollows of even-size celery ribs, and press them together in threes, making a roll. Chill, then slice across with a very sharp knife to make pinwheels.

- Use celery as an edible swizzle stick in tomato juice or other drinks.
- A simple but pleasant salad is made by finely slicing celery and adding thin flakes of Parmesan cheese, oil, lemon juice, and plenty of pepper.
- Always save celery leaves to use like an herb for flavor or to make a salad with watercress and sliced fennel dressed with vinaigrette. The thick base of the stalks can go into the stockpot.
- Stir-fry diagonally sliced celery until crisp-tender.
- Diced celery adds a nice crunch to all kinds of salads—egg, chicken, tuna, potato, and mixed vegetable—but be sure the celery pieces are smaller then the rest, and do not overuse it as a stretcher or its texture becomes overwhelming.
- For celery stuffing, combine equal amounts of finely chopped celery and milk or chicken broth. Add soft bread crumbs until mixture has the moisture you like. Season with sage, thyme, marjoram, and pepper. Add chopped lovage for an even stronger celery flavor.
- Add celery, diced or in chunks, to mixed pickles.

This unusual member of the cabbage family is sometimes called celery cabbage because the long, slender leaves and tender midribs of some varieties can be used like celery. With the popularity of quick wok cooking, much more Chinese cabbage is used today than five years ago.

You can choose among several kinds. Michihli (pe-tsai) grows 1½ feet tall in a romaine shape, with dark green leaves on the outside, gradually fading to white in the center of the head. Burpee Hybrid Chinese cabbage is more cylindrical in shape, with leaves, resembling Savoy cabbage, that fold inward at the top. Pak choi (or bok choy) cabbages look more like greenish white chard and have a pungent, almost bitter flavor. Pak choi matures faster than other Chinese cabbages and does not form a head.

Chinese cabbage seeds can be sown in a protected seed bed outside three months before the date of the usual first fall frost, pak choi two months before frost. Transplant the seedlings to a row, spacing them six to eight inches apart. Heads will not form if seeds are planted too soon—warm weather makes the plants go to seed.

When preparing either for salad or for cooking, always cut Chinese cabbage across the head and keep the tender top half separate from the thicker midribs near the base. The midribs require longer cooking and are often prepared as a separate cooked dish. The tender leaves can be added to a mixed green salad.

∘ Boiled Chinese Cabbage

Cut cabbage head across and add the thicker stem part to lightly salted boiling water. When almost tender, add the more tender leafy part of the cabbage. It will be done almost as soon as the water returns to a boil. Drain well in a strainer. Chop cabbage, add ¼ teaspoon celery seed and 2 tablespoons melted butter, and mix in well. Or try roasted sesame seeds or cumin seeds in place of celery seeds.

∘ Stir-Fried Chinese Cabbage

Heat 2 tablespoons oil in a skillet or wok and cook 4 thin slices of ginger root in it for 15 minutes over low heat. Remove ginger and add sliced Chinese cabbage, tougher parts first, and cook until well done. Salt lightly or use soy sauce.

° Chinese Cabbage Salad

Use the long Michihli type of Chinese cabbage. Rinse the head and leave it whole. Cut ½-inch slices across the middle of the head and place each slice, which has an attractive form, on an individual plate. I prefer Russian dressing on it, but you might like blue-cheese dressing made by crumbling cheese into oil and vinegar.

° Chinese Cabbage with Pineapple

Use the upper half of a head of Chinese cabbage. Slice it across in ½-inch strips and cut them so they are not so long that they would hang down from a fork. Wash and drain well until dry. Put cabbage in a bowl and add cut-up pineapple from a 10-ounce or 12-ounce can. (I prefer small pieces, but crushed will do.) Add some chopped fresh mint if you have it. Mix a dressing of two-thirds Old-Fashioned French Dressing (page 43) and one-third pineapple juice. Serve with cottage cheese.

Other Ideas for Chinese Cabbage

○ Thinly slice Chinese cabbage, add diced cucumber and diced green pepper, and toss with oil, vinegar, and soy sauce. Sprinkle with toasted sesame seeds.

○ Marinate shredded Chinese cabbage with shredded radishes and turnips and a generous amount of chopped fresh dill.

○ For an intriguing coleslaw with subtle flavor variations, shred as many cabbage-family vegetables as you have on hand: Chinese cabbage, pak choi, green and red cabbage, peeled broccoli stems, kohlrabi, turnips; add bits of cauliflower, kale, and turnip greens. Dress with a mustardy vinaigrette or mayonnaise dressing. Try adding freshly minced ginger to the mayonnaise.

○ The Japanese use Michihli cabbage (*hakusai*) in soups, stuff it like green cabbage leaves, and pickle it like sauerkraut (as do the Chinese) to add a piquant accent to a meal.

○ For a delicious rice with pieces of dark-green leaves and plump white stalks in it, cut ½ pound pak choi into 1-inch pieces, add 1 cup rice, 2 tablespoons oil or butter, and 2 cups water, and simmer, covered, until rice is tender.

○ Quickly stir-fry sliced Chinese cabbage, strips of filet mignon, snow peas, sliced mushrooms, and bamboo shoots for a westernized Oriental one-dish meal.

○ Add Chinese cabbage or pak choi leaves to a pot of mixed greens.

○ Chinese cabbage can be substituted for cabbage, celery, and chard in appropriate recipes. See discussions of these vegetables for ideas, and note recipes for Collard Leaf Rice Rolls.

Collards and kale are very much alike in the way they grow and are used. Both are vitamin rich. Collard plants will grow two feet tall. Their leaves are broad, blue-green, and slightly crumpled. Kale is more compact and usually has fine-toothed, curled, dark-green leaves, which from a distance resemble giant parsley, though some varieties have different colors and leaf shapes.

Collards do not have quite as strong a flavor as kale and will not withstand cold weather as well. I have picked kale in December when it was covered with snow and frozen stiff (if you do this, thaw it in water immediately). They are both cold-weather plants; collards will tolerate heat, but kale will shoot up to seed. They often winter over in my garden and produce delightful young green leaves in the spring before bolting into bloom.

Sow seeds in the garden in August, and thin out the rows as the plants grow (the thinnings are very tasty and tender), leaving plants one to one and a half feet apart to develop fully. When the plants are large the leaves are picked off as needed. As members of the cabbage family, kale and collards are susceptible to the same ailments. Treat cabbage worms with rotenone.

The midribs of collard and kale leaves are quite tough, so I always cut them out before cooking. I think the flavor is so strong they must be cooked in liquid rather than steamed, but do not boil them so long that they become slimy—cook only until tender, 15–20 minutes. Both collards and kale freeze well.

° Collard Leaf Rice Rolls

This is something you can make with leftover rice and a little bit of ground meat.

⅓-½ pound ground meat, such as bulk sausage, beef, or lamb
1 onion, finely chopped
1½ cups cooked rice
¼ teaspoon anise seed
¼ teaspoon salt, if needed

½ teaspoon poultry seasoning (if using beef or lamb)
8 large collard or Chinese cabbage leaves
4 fresh sorrel leaves, or lemon wedges

Cook the meat and onion in a fry pan, breaking the meat apart. If precooked meat is used, add 1½ tablespoons cooking oil. Add the rice, anise seed, salt, and poultry seasoning, and mix well.

Dip the collard or Chinese cabbage leaves in boiling water, holding on to the stem ends, until they are limp. Spread them on a work board, cut off the stems, and slit down the center rib of the leaf so it will roll easily. Tear or cut the leaves into pieces about 5 inches wide and 6 inches long (they can taper). Put 2 tablespoons of the rice mixture on bottom center of each leaf, put a 2-inch piece of sorrel leaf (if you have it) on top, and roll all this up in the leaf firmly, turning the sides in. Place the rolls tightly together on a steamer rack and heat for 15 minutes, uncovered, so they will keep their bright green color. If you didn't use sorrel, serve with lemon wedges. ***Serves 4.***

° *Thanksgiving Kale*

This is a quick, easily prepared green vegetable when the cook has many other things to do.

Gather kale from the garden. Wash in cold water and cut it up (kale does not chop as easily once cooked). Set in a strainer or spaghetti cooker in cold water. Twenty minutes before ready to serve, drain the kale. Then pour boiling water over it until it is covered. Cook over high heat with the lid off, about 20 minutes. When tender, drain and chop a bit. Drain again and press to extrude excess water. Add undiluted evaporated milk and chopped hard-boiled egg.   *Serves 8-10.*

Other Ideas for Collards and Kale

- ° Team kale and collard greens with hearty foods—pork chops, fried catfish, garlicky sausage, cornbread.
- ° Curly kale is pretty enough to use as a bed for raw vegetables or gelatin salads.
- ° Add shredded greens to bean soup or rice for color, texture, flavor, and nutrition.
- ° Top cooked greens with grated sharp Cheddar cheese and broil until melted.
- ° Simmer a ham hock for an hour, then add kale and small potatoes to absorb the salty flavor, cooking until tender.
- ° Southerners like to add bacon to the cooking water of kale and collards. I prefer cutting crumbled bacon and grated hard-boiled eggs on the greens after they are cooked, drained, and chopped.
- ° Portuguese use kale to make caldo verde (green broth). Make your own version by combining mashed potatoes, sliced cooked spicy sausages (such as chorizo), and finely shredded kale. Add broth and some olive oil and cook gently until kale is tender.
- ° Cook kale or collards until tender, chop fine, and fold in sour cream and a little nutmeg.
- ° Use kale or collards instead of cabbage or spinach in cooked

dishes, but cook greens longer—see discussions of cabbage and spinach ideas.

- Sauté kale in oil with red pepper flakes and chopped garlic. Add a cup or two of water and boil covered for 10 minutes, then uncovered until water evaporates.

I think I have been asked more questions about the Jerusalem artichoke than about any other vegetable, perhaps because its name creates a lot of confusion: it doesn't look like and is not an artichoke but resembles a strange, knobby, small potato. Fortunately for me, D. G. Routley wrote an excellent article on Jerusalem artichokes for the *American Horticulturist* (Vol. 56, No. 4, 1977), from which I have taken these historical facts. It is a native plant of North America used by the Indians and is really a species of sunflower, which produces tubers on its roots. We can probably blame the early-seventeenth-century explorer Samuel de Champlain for the confusion, because he described them as having the flavor of artichokes.

The plants are strong and produce many tubers, so it did not take long before these so-called artichokes were growing everywhere in Europe. In Spain they were called *gérasol* and in Italy *girasole*, which became corrupted in English to "Jerusalem." So now we have Jerusalem artichokes.

Jerusalem artichokes need little care and are not particular about soil. Set out the tubers in early spring, preferably in a bed by themselves. They grow as tall as the sunflowers to which they are related, so they may need staking. You must wait until after the first frost to harvest them. Wear gloves to pull up the roots—the stems are spiny—or leave them in the ground over winter and dig them in the spring. They store well if kept just above freezing in damp sand.

I definitely do not advise just anyone to plant Jerusalem artichokes, as they need space, take over the area, spread, and are hard to get rid of. But they are fun to have. My grandfather grew them in a corner of his backyard in Hartford. I have been trying to duplicate the delicious raw pickles my grandmother made, but have not yet found a recipe that tastes so good.

Jerusalem artichokes appear in the market in late fall and early spring, sometimes under the name "sunchokes." Cold weather changes the chemical structure of the sugars in the tubers and makes them sweeter and more digestible. They are a safe vegetable for diabetics, a good substitute for potatoes, since they have a low glucose content and the fructose in them allows them to be digested without insulin.

Jerusalem artichokes should be scrubbed to clean them, but do not peel before cooking. When eating them raw, peel if you like (though the skin is edible) and immerse in acidulated water until ready to use, or they will discolor.

○ Pan-Browned Jerusalem Artichokes

Scrub chokes and cut into slices or cubes and brown in butter or margarine for a few minutes for a substitute for hash-browned potatoes. I've found they have a slight laxative effect when eaten in quantity, and they can also cause flatulence, so don't overeat until you know how your system takes to them.

○ Mashed Jerusalem Artichokes

Jerusalem artichokes cook very quickly. Boil with skins on in slightly salted water with a teaspoon of oil for 15 minutes. Peel and mash. Add butter and chopped parsley, sorrel, or chives for seasoning. For a better texture, you can also mash chokes with potatoes.

Other Ideas for Jerusalem Artichokes

○ Raw artichokes have a nutty, slightly sweet flavor. Add them
   to mixed salads or add slices to a tray of raw vegetables.
○ Raw chokes are a good substitute for water chestnuts in
   Oriental dishes. Add them just before serving to retain their
   crispness.
○ Peel and chunk chokes and simmer in water with a squeeze of
   lemon just until tender, about 10 minutes. Drain and dress
   with lemon juice, olive oil, and lots of chopped parsley. Add
   some cubed avocado if you like, and sprinkle with crumbled
   bacon.
○ To make Palestine soup, cook chokes with potatoes, onions,
   celery, and an herb bouquet. Purée and add milk, cream, or
   butter to taste.
○ Gently cook thinly sliced chokes in butter for 5 minutes. Add
   chicken stock to cover, simmer until tender, then add heavy
   cream, a little nutmeg, and a squeeze of lemon juice.
○ The French boil chokes in milk flavored with an onion stuck
   with a clove, then drain the chokes, dip them in batter, and
   fry them.
○ Grate carrots and sauté them gently while you grate chokes
   into acidulated water. When carrots are almost tender, squeeze
   chokes dry, add them to carrots, and stir-fry until tender.
○ To make simple pickles, boil chokes for a few minutes, then
   cover with wine vinegar. Add spices or herbs to taste.
○ John Goodyer, the pioneer planter of Jerusalem artichokes,
   said in 1621 that some people "bake them in pies, putting in
   Marrow, Dates, Ginger, Raisons of the sun, Sacke [sherry],
   etc." You might want to try this when the choke crop
   proliferates.
○ See recipe for Jerusalem Artichoke Relish.

The Scots have their cockaleekie, the French their potage parmentier, the Welsh their leek soup—and the Americans? They generally ignore this elegant member of the onion family, or else pay exorbitant prices for it, because it is practically a scarce vegetable here. If you are patient—leeks take four months to mature—you can have your own, fresh and tender from the garden, from September through winter and early spring at little expense or trouble—if you live where temperatures do not drop below 10° F. and mulch the bed to keep the soil from freezing hard.

Leek seedlings are so fine that they are best started indoors, two months before the last expected heavy frost in the North. Germination is very slow. When the seedlings are four inches high, pinch off the tips to encourage strong development. When they are about six inches high, move them to the garden; space about five inches apart.

Insects are not a problem with leeks unless they are grown in heavy soil, where a small white worm gets at their roots. They are trouble-free growing in soil rich in organic matter and fertilized every four weeks.

Tall tender white leaks are grown in a shallow trench and earth is piled around them when they get as thick as a pencil (but it is not necessary to do this). Unfortunately this gets grit into them, which the cook has to get out. To do so, remove the first two or three outer leaves, then make a two-inch slit lengthwise down the leek. Hold it under the faucet so that the running water flows between the leaves and forces the grit out. Pull the leaves apart gently. Should they separate too much, use toothpicks to hold them together while cooking.

Even though leeks are cousins of the onion, their flavor is mild and sweet even when they are mature. In fact, finger-size leeks are wonderful raw, eaten like scallions, and they don't affect your breath! Mature leeks take 15–20 minutes to boil tender.

○ *Leeks au Gratin*

Peel the outer leaves off 6 leeks and wash leeks thoroughly. Cut the tender inner stalk into 4-inch-long pieces. At the base, cut only the roots off so leaves are still held together. Parboil on a rack in seasoned chicken stock until a fork penetrates easily. Drain, saving the stock, and place leeks in a heatproof vegetable dish.

Make a cream sauce: Combine 2 tablespoons flour and ⅓ cup powdered milk, add ½ cup milk, and mix. Add 1 tablespoon butter and ½ cup hot stock in which leeks were cooked. Cook over low heat until thickened. Pour over leeks. Sprinkle seasoned bread crumbs and grated Parmesan cheese on top. Dot with butter and place dish under broiler for a minute. **Serves 4.**

Other Ideas for Leeks

- ○ Cook leeks just until tender, drain, and chill in vinaigrette. Olives are a good addition, and grated hard-boiled egg makes an attractive topping.
- ○ The Greeks cook leeks with tomatoes, onions, and celery in chicken broth until tender, then add oregano, oil, and lemon juice to the broth, reduce it, pour it over the leeks, and chill to serve as a salad.
- ○ Cook young leeks until tender, chill, and wrap a thin slice of smoky ham around each leek. Serve with mustardy mayonnaise.
- ○ For simple leek soup, chop leeks, sauté in butter for 5 minutes, stir in flour, then broth, and cook until tender. Purée and add milk or cream. For Welsh and Flemish soup, add potatoes; for

Scotch cockaleekie, some oatmeal. Add some thinly sliced tender green stalk for color before serving.

○ Boil young leeks with pearl onions and add sour cream or serve with a mushroom sauce.

○ To braise leeks, remove tops and roots, place leeks in a baking dish, and cover with sliced carrot, minced celery, parsley, and thyme. Add beef broth, cover tightly, and bake at 350° F. for about 45 minutes. For leeks Provençal, braise with garlic and tomatoes.

○ Soften chopped leeks in butter and add them to quiche—good in a ham-and-cheese tart.

○ Save the upper tender green part of leeks to add to soups—a little fresh green vegetable added to canned soups gives a homemade touch. Even the tougher leek leaves can be added to the stockpot for flavor.

○ Leeks have been called "poor man's asparagus" (though not in the United States), and slender young leeks can be substituted in some asparagus recipes (see discussion of asparagus for ideas).

People either like parsnips very much or they dislike them. Once when a newspaper reporter asked my husband if he had a favorite vegetable—as marigolds were his favorite flower—he thought a minute and then said, "Candied parsnips." The newspaper column brought a flood of requests for how to cook them and letters from other parsnip lovers.

Parsnips are slow-growing, four to five months to maturity, so the seeds are sown directly in the garden in early June. They need deeply worked, loose, light soil for best growth of their long roots. As the seed germinates very slowly, it is helpful to mix a fast-germinating seed such as radish or lettuce with it to mark the row. Or, since the seeds require wet soil for germination, put a board over the row where parsnips are planted, leave it there for two weeks, then raise the board for a few days before removing it. Plants should be thinned to at least 4 inches apart. They grow slowly in the heat of summer, but when the weather gets cooler they fill out. An extra feeding of 5-10-10 fertilizer in August will improve the roots. Insects leave them alone.

The flavor of the roots is improved by frost, which changes the carbohydrates to sugar—even freezing won't hurt them. When I bring in the roots I give them a good scrubbing. I find it easier to peel them after cooking.

○ Candied Parsnips

Scrub and boil 1 pound parsnips in salted water until a fork goes through easily, at least 45 minutes. Drain and remove the paper-thin skin. Cut across into ¾-inch-thick slices. If the center core is hard, remove it and cut into long pieces instead of round ones.

Rub a shallow ovenproof vegetable dish with butter. Mix ¾ cup brown sugar (not packed) with ¼ teaspoon nutmeg and ¼ teaspoon cinnamon. Layer parsnips in the dish and sprinkle sugar mixture over each layer. Dot with 3 tablespoons butter or margarine. Cover with aluminum foil and bake in a 375° oven for 30 minutes. Remove foil, baste the parsnips, and bake uncovered for 15 minutes more, basting twice. **Serves 5.**

°Parsnip Fritters

This is basically Mrs. Rorer's recipe, from *How to Cook Vegetables*. If you wish a bit of a mystery flavor, add ¼ teaspoon mace to the parsnips.

4 good-size parsnips, well scrubbed	**1 tablespoon flour**
	1 egg, well beaten
Salt and white pepper	**2 tablespoons oil or drippings**

Boil parsnips in salted water until tender and put through food mill or ricer. Add flour, beaten egg, ½ teaspoon salt, and a dash of white pepper. Mix well and make into small round cakes. Heat oil or drippings in fry pan, add cakes, and turn when brown on one side. Drain on brown paper when done. *Serves 4.*

Other Ideas for Parsnips

- Add slivers of raw parsnip to a vegetable platter and serve with dip.
- The flavor of parsnips is complemented by dill, chervil, ginger, and mace.
- I serve parsnips with poultry or ham—not with fish or beef, and not with winter squash or starchy vegetables.
- To bring out the sweet, nutty flavor of parsnips, rub them with butter and bake at 350° F. for about 45 minutes. Even better, bake them along with a pork roast.
- Make parsnip chips or French fries by cutting them in appropriate shape and frying in deep fat.
- If you are ever served "mock lobster," it's cooked parsnip chunks mixed with mayonnaise, and while not lobster it's quite good.
- For scalloped parsnips, dice cooked parsnips and layer with bread crumbs, green pepper, and onions. Pour on a cheese sauce and bake at 350° F. for 30 minutes.
- Mash parsnips as you would potatoes, moistening with butter and cream, or sour cream with dill, or softened cream cheese and some ground ginger.

○ An unusual stuffing for Rock Cornish hens or pork chops is made by cooking shredded parsnips, chopped celery leaves or lovage, and grated onion in plenty of butter, then combining with bread crumbs, cardamom, mace, and pepper.

○ If you've been looking for a recipe for parsnip wine, here's how you make it: Boil 1 peck parsnips in 2 gallons water for 2 hours. Strain and add 6 pounds sugar. Cool, add 1 cake yeast, and set aside to ferment for 1 week. Strain, cork and place in a dark place for 6 months.

○ Parsnips can be prepared in ways suitable for carrots, potatoes, and kohlrabi. See discussions of these vegetables for ideas.

Though potatoes today are among the world's chief food crops, at one time they were considered poisonous because the herbalists classified them in the deadly nightshade family. They are native to South America and are said to have been taken to the European continent by Spanish explorers and to England by Sir Walter Raleigh around 1580. There is some question about whether the colonists brought potatoes with them to America or whether the Virginia settlers got them from the Indians.

Potatoes need rich, acid soil and plenty of water. They grow best at temperatures around 55–75° F., so are not a hot-climate vegetable. The potato "seed" is actually a piece of the potato tuber with an eye in it from which a sprout grows. Pieces of potato with at least two eyes each should be planted, eyes up, and covered with four or five inches of soil.

Always store potatoes, especially new ones, in the dark; in the light they can become green, an indication of the presence of poisonous solanine. Raw potatoes should not be frozen—at temperatures below freezing their starch turns to sugar—but some cooked potato dishes freeze well.

"The vegetable kingdom affords no food more wholesome, more easily procured, easily prepared, or less expensive, than the potato. Yet although this most useful vegetable is dressed almost every day, in almost every family, for one plate of potatoes that comes to the table as it should come, ten are spoiled." This is a quote from my husband's grandmother's cookbook, *The Cook's Own Book*, by "A Boston Housekeeper," published in 1854. A like opinion is expressed by Mrs. Rorer, the principal of the Philadelphia Cooking School, in her *How to Cook Vegetables*, published in 1892. The lament today might be that, because of the way potatoes are dried, frozen, and otherwise commercially processed, so few people enjoy the splendor of a fresh potato, simply prepared and served with herb-scented butter.

The most nutritious part of the potato is just under the skin, so potatoes that are not peeled are a better food. The longer a peeled potato is in water, the less food value it has, so please do not let potatoes stand in water for long before and especially after boiling.

○ Mashed Potatoes

The contents of baked potatoes can be mashed and put back into the skins (I often choose to do this when entertaining, for the potato stays fluffy in a warm oven), but you must peel potatoes before cooking to make good, tasty mashed potatoes. To make fluffy mashed potatoes, boil "old" potatoes that have a dry, floury texture (unlike new waxy ones); pour the water off the potatoes as soon as a fork penetrates them easily. Return pot containing potatoes to a warm stove burner and break the potatoes apart with a fork. The heat forces the steam out of the potatoes and they literally fall apart with only a little mashing needed. This is the time to season with salt and butter and a little milk or cream if desired. Do not cover mashed potatoes—they will become soggy. To keep them hot until serving time, place the pot of mashed potatoes in a pan of hot water on the stove. Sometimes mashed potatoes get stuck to the bottom of the pot. When this happens, run *cold* water into the pot immediately after serving and the stuck potato will come off easily.

∘ *New Potatoes*

There is nothing like a small new potato, fresh from the earth, boiled or steamed in its jacket. Young red, thin-skinned potatoes are also a nice change when they come on the market. Wash and boil them with skins on until a fork pierces them easily. Then cut them into quarters and put in an ovenproof dish. Dot generously with butter and sprinkle with parsley, mint, or dill. Put under the broiler for a few minutes. Let each person salt them to his or her own taste. Or serve with lemon butter—wonderful with asparagus served alongside the potatoes.

∘ *Baked Potatoes*

Not everyone knows how to serve a good baked potato, and this includes most restaurants, particularly the ones that wrap them in foil. The steam inside the potato must be given a chance to get out for the insides to be white and fluffy. I bake well-washed potatoes, preferably dry, floury ones such as Russets, at 375° F. for 30 minutes, then pierce them twice with a fork and continue baking until they will split or soften with pressure. A crispy skin is a special treat.

° Scalloped Potatoes

Slice peeled raw potatoes (or, if you wish, potatoes that have been boiled in their skins until half-cooked, then skins removed) into a well-buttered baking dish. Make a layer about 1 inch thick. Dust flour over it and dot with butter. Cover with a layer of thinly sliced onion. Make a second and third layer. Shake salt and paprika over top, dot with butter, and pour milk to within ½ inch of the top of the potatoes. The rim of the dish should be at least 1 inch higher than the potatoes. Put a pan under the dish, as milk has a way of boiling over. Cover and bake in a 325° oven for 20–30 minutes, then uncover and continue baking until soft. Just before serving, brown lightly under the broiler if not already brown.

° Potato Salad

Boil 4 medium-size potatoes, preferably waxy-textured ones, in their skins, peel while hot, so they dry out a bit, and cut into pieces. Shake some salt on them and put in a large measuring cup. Add one-third as much sliced celery as potato, ¼ cup chopped celery leaves, and chopped onion to your taste. I prefer scallions—not too many, maybe ¼ cup—to onion. Add ½-⅓ cup chopped mint leaves. Mix a dressing of one-third mayonnaise and two-thirds oil and vinegar. Pour ½ cup over everything and let stand for about 1 hour. Taste before serving, as the salad usually needs a little more dressing. Serve on a bed of lettuce. This sometimes tastes better the second day.

Variation: Celeriac may be substituted for the potatoes. Scrub the roots and boil until tender, about 30 minutes. Peel and discard all fibrous pieces. Then proceed with recipe above. **Serves 6.**

Other Ideas for Potatoes

° Spring potato salad is lovely to look at and taste: combine sliced cooked new potatoes, peas, asparagus, and the first thinnings of carrots, turnips, and radishes in a light, lemony vinaigrette or mayonnaise.

- Make thick potato soup by thinning mashed potatoes with butter and milk or cream. Sprinkle with crumbled bacon and chopped parsley.
- For Portuguese potato soup, cook grated potatoes in beef broth, add finely chopped watercress, and egg yolks to thicken, and sprinkle with grated cheese.
- The French sometimes add meat juices to mashed potatoes instead of milk. Another idea is to spin fresh herbs in the blender with liquid and add to mashed potatoes. Or add puréed vegetables of your choice.
- Cook sliced floury-textured potatoes and pearl onions with a bay leaf, some butter, and dry white wine to cover.
- Swiss rösti is usually made with potatoes that have been boiled the previous day and kept overnight (traditionally in the snow) to dry out a little They are then grated, fried gently in butter, and inverted to serve with the golden crust on top.
- For a cooling raïta to serve with curry, combine chopped cooked potatoes with cumin, coriander, and yogurt. Chill before serving.
- Cook whole potatoes in a pot of ham and greens to soak up the salty flavors.
- For potatoes Romanoff, combine cubed cooked potatoes, cottage cheese, sour cream, garlic, and scallions. Put in buttered casserole, sprinkle with grated Cheddar, and bake at 350° F. for 30 minutes.
- Combine cubed cooked potatoes with cream of tomato soup. Put in a buttered casserole and bake at 350° F. for 30 minutes.
- Rub peeled potatoes with butter, place around a beef or pork roast, and bake with the roast.
- Vegetarians cook potato peels with onion, carrots, celery, and herbs for a tasty, nutritious nonmeat soup base.
- Use leftover mashed potatoes to make patties or shepherd's pie or to thicken soups or sauces; leftover boiled potatoes are useful for hash browns, corned beef hash, or vegetable salads.

The pumpkin, a tropical American plant, was first grown for its edible seeds, and today you can buy a variety called Lady Godiva which produces seeds without hulls. You can also select varieties for their huge size, such as Big Max, or for Halloween carving, such as Jack-O'-Lantern. But if you want pumpkin flesh for cooking, it is best to grow a meaty, sweet variety such as Small Sugar. Triple Treat is an all-around good pumpkin for carving, pies, or seeds.

Most pumpkins take almost four months to develop and the plants spread widely, so they are not a good vegetable for small gardens—although you can buy Cinderella, a bush-type pumpkin that matures in ninety-five days. Seeds are sown directly in the garden when the soil has become warm. Plant a few seeds in a hill and cover with two inches of soil. Thin to one strong plant when seedlings have developed. The hills should be spaced at least five feet apart. One vine will produce only two or three good-size pumpkins.

Harvest pumpkins just before the first frost or when their shells are firm and their color bright orange. (Do not, however, discard green ones that aren't ready by frost—they won't be very sweet, but you can use them in any way you use winter squash.) Leave on a small portion of the pumpkin stem, and cure the fruit about ten days at about 80° F. to harden the shells. Store in a dry spot at 45–50° F.

To cook pumpkin, cut it in chunks, removing seeds and fiber, and steam vigorously for 30–40 minutes. Or cut pumpkin in half and bake cut side down on a tray at 400° F. until tender, 45–60 minutes. Scrape soft flesh away from the skin. For smoothest texture, purée in a food mill. Pumpkin purée freezes well.

◦ *Pumpkin Seeds*

Scoop the pumpkin seeds out and separate the fibers from them while they are moist. Spread the seeds out in one layer on paper plates to dry in a warm, airy place for about a week. A quick way to roast them is to heat 1 tablespoon cooking oil in a frying pan, add a thin layer of seeds, and stir gently. Partially cover, as some seeds pop. When the seeds swell, remove them at once and dry on absorbent paper. Salt if desired.

Slightly oiled seeds may also be roasted on a cookie sheet in a 350° oven for about 15 minutes.

◦ *Pumpkin Pie*

Many families have their own traditional pumpkin pie recipe. I don't, because I prefer to use butternut or buttercup squash in pies—I think they have firmer, more tasty flesh. Pumpkin is not one of my favorite pies, and usually the bottom crust is heavy. To avoid this, I advise baking the crust for 20 minutes on the low shelf in the oven before adding the pumpkin custard. The Burpee tradition is for each person to shake sweet sherry on his portion when served.

Other Ideas for Pumpkin

- ◦ Make pumpkin soup by adding cream or milk to puréed pumpkin. Mix in puréed carrots, or add sautéed leeks, onions, and celery.
- ◦ Shred raw pumpkin and quickly stir-fry it in butter.
- ◦ In New England, a delicious casserole is made by combining mashed pumpkin, cream sauce, diced ham, and grated Cheddar. This is topped with cracker crumbs, dots of butter, and more cheese and baked at 350° F. for 30 minutes.
- ◦ Thinly slice cooked pumpkin and layer it with cooked rice and minced green peppers in a casserole. Pour on a cheese sauce and bake until bubbly.
- ◦ Cut a lid off a small pumpkin and remove seeds and fiber. Fill

pumpkin with your favorite cooked rice mixture (curried rice is good, or a pilaf with mushrooms), replace lid, and bake at 425° F. for about 1 hour—pumpkin will begin to char and feel soft to the touch. Serve by scooping out rice with the soft pumpkin flesh.

° Add diced pumpkin and raisins to a wild rice stuffing for Cornish game hens.

° Ground pumpkin seeds have been used for centuries in Mexican cooking. To make a piquant dip for tortillas, toast pumpkin seeds until brown and crisp, then grind to a powder with salt in a spice grinder. Add chopped cooked tomatoes, chopped coriander leaves and chives, and fresh hot green chili peppers to taste.

° Add pumpkin purée, a little dark rum, and pie spices to your favorite recipe for vanilla ice cream.

° Pumpkin can be substituted in almost any recipe for winter squash—see pages 178–185 for ideas.

Mr. Burpee once thought that he might be able to increase the sales of salsify if he mentioned in the catalog that herbalists of old claimed that eating salsify improved a man's virility. Prudence kept him from doing so. A close relative of salsify, scorzonera, sometimes called black salsify because of the black skin on the roots, was considered a powerful tonic in the Middle Ages.

The salsify plant has long grasslike leaves which have a milky sap. Because of its long, thin roots, it should be grown in loamy or well-dug soil. Seeds are sown in the garden in spring—they will not germinate in heat. Thin the plants to three inches apart. The young plants you have pulled out are good in salads or boiled as greens in water with a little lemon juice. Rabbits love the young leaves.

Salsify requires frequent watering for the first two months, and it is best not to disturb the soil around the roots. A side dressing of a 5-10-10 fertilizer is advisable in midsummer.

The roots are dug (you cannot pull them out) in the fall after the weather has turned cold, or they may be left in the garden to be dug in early winter or very early spring if the rabbits cannot get to them.

Salsify roots have a slightly mealy texture and a mild flavor that some people think suggests oysters and others like me do not. I believe the association with oysters comes from their color, not the flavor.

Salsify will become rusty when cut raw, so immediately immerse peeled pieces in acidulated water. It has more flavor when cooked first and then peeled and cut into pieces.

Cook salsify only until tender—do not let it become mushy. I serve it as a substitute for potato.

Preventing Discolored Vegetables

The French cook vegetables such as salsify and celeriac, which darken if exposed to air, in a *blanc*—simply water to which a tablespoon or so of flour and some lemon juice or vinegar have been added. This prevents the grayish color that some vegetables acquire in cooking.

○ *Creamed Salsify*

Boil salsify whole for 45 minutes, peel, and slice across. Keep covered, or add immediately to Basic White Sauce (page 30), 1 cup sauce for 2 cups sliced salsify. Add a rounded tablespoon of snipped parsley or chives for each cup of sauce. You can also make a sauce with 2 tablespoons butter, 2 tablespoons flour, ½ cup powdered milk, and 1 cup clam broth. Sprinkle a little paprika on top when serving to add color.

○ *Salsify Fritters or Mock Oysters*

2 eggs, well beaten	1 teaspoon chopped chervil
1 tablespoon melted butter	(optional)
1 teaspoon salt	3 cups mashed cooked salsify
Pinch of white pepper	¾ cup flour
	1 teaspoon baking powder

Add eggs, butter, salt, pepper, and chervil (if you like) to salsify. Sift flour and baking powder into mixture and mix well. Drop a tablespoon at a time into deep oil or fat heated to 380° F. Drain on brown paper when browned.   *Serves 6.*

Other Ideas for Salsify

- ○ You can have fun experimenting with the use of different herbs with salsify, whether it is creamed, boiled, or sautéed in butter. I suggest a combination of sorrel and thyme. Try adding a little at first until you get the flavor you want.
- ○ Add parboiled cut up salsify to baked scallop or oyster casseroles.
- ○ Add young salsify shoots raw to salads when you thin the planting row.
- ○ Cook salsify (along with other winter vegetables if you like), slice, and dress with vinaigrette.
- ○ Dice cooked salsify, fold with lemony mayonnaise and chopped anchovies, and garnish with black olives.
- ○ Use salsify in place of a starch in a meal. It goes well with

ham when creamed. Serve with chicken or lamb and add a green vegetable.

○ Cook salsify chunks until tender, soak in lemon juice and oil for 30 minutes, then dip in batter and deep-fry. Serve with tartar sauce.

○ Sauté roots cut lengthwise in oil and butter until almost tender, add chopped parsley, minced garlic, and some tomato sauce, and reduce slightly.

○ For glazed salsify, scrape the roots and drop immediately into acidulated water. Boil under tender, drain, and sauté in butter and sugar, rolling and shaking until salsify is nicely coated.

○ Purée or mash cooked salsify, beating in butter and a little cream. If you like, sprinkle with cheese and run under broiler.

What is the difference between a pumpkin and a squash? My husband said he heard a seasoned salesman reply, "If you throw up a pumpkin it comes down a squash." Well, it's not quite that simple. It is the stem of the fruit that gives the answer, not its appearance. If the stem is hard and has ridges it is a pumpkin, if soft and round it is a squash. But in our garden-vegetable nomenclature this characteristic is disregarded, and common usage and appearance prevail.

Plants of the late-harvested squashes all used to grow on large, sprawling vines, but plant breeders have now developed some bush types of the smaller varieties of winter squash. However, the fruits are apt to be smaller, too. Because they have to be left to mature, winter squash are not as prolific as summer squash. Usually the plants of larger squash used for winter storage produce only three or four fruits.

Seeds are sown directly in the garden after the soil has warmed up and all danger of frost is over. They do best in fertile soil with plenty of moisture. I plant mine in groups of five or six seeds in a circle ten inches in diameter and four feet apart if bush types, five or six feet if vining type. I put Hotkaps over them to keep the birds away. Water the soil before adding the Hotkaps. When the plants have grown two inches tall, in about two weeks, I pull out all but two or three per group and remove the Hotkaps. Later I select only two plants per group to continue growing.

Some of the late squash, such as butternut, can be eaten in the green stage, but they have a very different flavor—sweeter and firmer than summer squash but not as mellow as when mature.

Harvest mature squash with stem attached to prevent rotting at the base. Store them in a cool, dry place. They do not lose quality after picking as most vegetables do—their vitamin A content is actually increased during storage. Hubbard squash can be stored as long as six months, others somewhat less, depending on the thickness of their skins. Squash purée freezes well.

There are differences in flavor and texture among the hard-skinned winter squashes, and gardeners have their preferences. I like the taste and nutty texture of buttercup squash, but as a substitute for candied sweet potatoes I use butternut, which can be cut in nice pieces. I think each type of winter squash is appropriate for a particular use, so I am giving recipes for each.

Acorn Squash

This, in my opinion, has the firmest flesh of the late squashes and is best prepared as individual servings. Usually one squash provides two servings. Larger squash can be cut into thirds.

Wash the squash and cut following the natural lines from stem to tip. Remove seeds and strings. Use a flat ovenproof dish or broiler pan at least 1½ inches deep. Put an inch of water in the pan and add a teaspoon of salt. Lay the squash in the pan cut side down. Cook in a 350° oven for 30 minutes, or longer if the squash is large.

Remove from oven and pour off remaining water. Line the pan with foil, so it will be easy to clean, and replace squash cut sides up. Pierce the flesh with a fork all over so that seasonings penetrate. Rub butter or margarine generously all over the flesh. Shake in some cinnamon and nutmeg and pour dark corn syrup over the flesh. Put some brown sugar on the top rims. Return to 350° oven and bake for 40 minutes. As the squash bakes, a pool of seasoned syrup will form in the hollows. Baste the insides at least twice with the syrup.

For a meal in one dish, bake as in first step above, then baste with sherry if you like and stuff with a creamed chicken or turkey filling. Top with crumbs, brown, then add a dab of cranberry sauce.

Or brush the squash with mustard, sprinkle with brown sugar, and fill with creamed ham.

Acorn squash is also good filled and baked with chutney and diced apples.

Buttercup Squash

Turban-shaped buttercup squash is more mealy and nutty than other winter squashes and perhaps also sweeter. It is my choice for mashed squash and "pumpkin" pie, but it can also be cut in sections and prepared the same way as acorn squash.

∘ Mashed Buttercup Squash

Wash whole squash, put it on a baking pan, and bake in a 375° oven until soft, about 45 minutes. Cut open while hot to let steam out. Remove seeds and strings and, when a bit cooler, scoop out the flesh with a spoon and mash it. Season with salt and butter. If you wish, add ¼ teaspoon nutmeg or allspice. If serving with cold lamb, season with ½ teaspoon grated orange rind and butter instead of spices. Mashed squash is good with anything except fish.

Butternut Squash

Butternut squash, which looks like a pear-shaped club, is getting to be the most popular of winter squashes. The shape, small seed cavity, and solid texture of the orange flesh are the good points of butternut squash—in addition to its flavor, of course. Also, it is possible to peel it. You can use any sweet potato or pumpkin recipe with this squash.

○*Candied Butternut Squash*

Boil or bake the squash whole until a fork pierces it easily. Cool and cut the squash lengthwise, scoop out the seeds and strings, and peel. Cut across into ¾-inch pieces and shake salt over them. Arrange pieces overlapping at an angle in a well-buttered shallow ovenproof serving dish or casserole and shake nutmeg or mace and cinnamon over them. Or use nutmeg and grated orange rind. Cover generously with brown sugar and pour melted butter over all. Bake in a 325° oven for 30 minutes or more. If the squash seems a little dry, pour apple juice over it.

○*Butternut Squash Polynesian Medley*

I thought up this recipe for a garden-club luncheon in October. They always expect something different when they come to Fordhook, and I try not to disappoint them. I served this dish with a mixed green salad and rolls, and for dessert we had lemon chiffon pie made by a co-hostess.

2 cups unsweetened pineapple
    chunks with juice
8 thin slices fresh ginger
3 tablespoons oil
2 tablespoons light-brown sugar
3 cups diced tender ham, or Spam
    or Treat (one 16-ounce can)

4 cups peeled raw butternut
    squash cut in 1-inch cubes
¼ cup chopped sweet red peppers
    (once I used a small piece of hot
    pepper and it gave a nice
    surprise)
1 teaspoon salt, or less
2 teaspoons soy sauce
1½ teaspoons cornstarch

Drain the pineapple, reserving ⅔ cup of the juice. Simmer the ginger in the oil for 10 minutes. Remove the ginger and stir in brown sugar. Add the meat, squash, pineapple chunks, and peppers. Stir and cook until squash is warm through, about 15 minutes, but squash should still be firm. Mix reserved pineapple juice with remaining ingredients and stir into the squash mixture. Cook for 5 minutes.   *Serves 5-6*

Hubbard Squash

This squash has a nice nutty flavor when not cooked too long or served too moist. It is large and keeps for a long time, and is often used in place of pumpkin in New England, as it is a better keeper. Its very hard shell, its only bad feature, has to be cut before cooking. Scoop out the seeds and strings and cook pieces in boiling water for 30 minutes, or until soft. Immediately drain and allow steam to get out of the flesh, so do not cover. Remove flesh from the skin. Mash and season for either a side dish or a pie, or use in muffins and cake. Freeze what you do not need to use right away. When serving as a vegetable, add a little allspice or mace if you wish.

Spaghetti Squash

Spaghetti squash got its name because of the appearance of the flesh, not its flavor. Some people use it in place of spaghetti because of its lower calorie content, but I think tomato sauces kill the fine, delicate flavor of the squash. To keep this flavor, cook the squash whole.

The squash must reach a certain stage of ripeness for the flesh to separate into "spaghetti." When it has changed from light green to greenish yellow, test with your fingernail. If it cannot be penetrated or bruised, the squash is ready to pick. Mine are at their prime in late August. Later in the season the spaghetti-like pulp is drier.

○ Basic Spaghetti Squash

Place whole squash in pan and bake for 45 minutes at 350° F. Or pierce the squash in four or five places and put in a pot of boiling water. Cover and boil for 30–45 minutes. When a fork pierces it easily, it is done.

Take squash out of oven or water and cut it in half across the center. Scoop out seeds and stringy fibers. Then take a large spoon and scoop out flesh into a bowl. Using two forks, pull apart the flesh so that it separates into spaghetti-like strands. These should be slightly crisp. (If it doesn't separate, the squash was either too young or not cooked quite enough.) Put the squash in a heavy pot or double boiler, season, and heat. This extra heating will help fibers to separate. If you have too much squash for one meal, refrigerate the extra before heating.

Seasoning: Your selection will depend on what else you are serving for the meal. For about 3 cups cooked squash, the basic seasoning is:

½ teaspoon salt   1½ tablespoons butter
¼ teaspoon nutmeg

Choices to add to above:

1 teaspoon lemon rind when   ½ teaspoon mace when serving
  serving with fish   with beef
1 teaspoon grated fresh orange
  rind and 1 rounded tablespoon
  brown sugar when serving with
  poultry or ham

Freezing Spaghetti Squash

All prepared dishes of spaghetti squash freeze well. They should thaw first if they are to be heated. Frozen spaghetti squash salads can be eaten cold but are also good heated.

° *Sherried Spaghetti Squash*

2 cups crisp-cooked spaghetti
squash
2 rounded tablespoons brown
sugar
½ teaspoon salt
1 rounded tablespoon cornstarch

¾ cup orange juice
½ tablespoon grated fresh orange
peel or 1 teaspoon dried
3 tablespoons butter
½ cup dry sherry
¼ cup raisins, preferably golden

Keep spaghetti squash warm in a double boiler. In a saucepan mix brown sugar, salt, cornstarch, orange juice, and grated peel. Cook until it boils, then add remaining ingredients, gently mixing in the squash. Turn up heat to make hot, or heat in a covered casserole in the oven, stirring occasionally.   *Serves 4.*

° *Sweet-and-Sour Spaghetti Squash*

Serve this with hot pork or any cold meats.

1 spaghetti squash
¾ cup white or cider vinegar
¾ cup sugar
¼ teaspoon turmeric
⅛ teaspoon ground cloves
½ teaspoon mustard seed
¼ teaspoon celery seed

1 teaspoon salt
½ cup minced celery heart and
leaves
1 tablespoon chopped parsley
1 teaspoon minced hot red pepper
(optional)

Pierce spaghetti squash in 4 or 5 places and boil whole for 30–45 minutes. While squash is boiling, combine vinegar, sugar, turmeric, cloves, mustard seed, celery seed, and salt. Simmer for 2 minutes and let cool. This makes 1 cup marinade. (Leftover marinade is good to use on beets or brush on boiled ham).

When squash is cooked, prepare it as directed on page 182. Measure out 3 cups of it and add ¼ cup of the marinade (you might like more), celery, parsley, and hot pepper (if you like).   *Serves 5-6.*

°Spaghetti Squash Salad

You can use any seasoned oil-and-vinegar dressing for spaghetti squash salad. (Do not use a creamy dressing or one with a strong garlic flavor that would kill the taste of the squash.) The following salad has pleased my guests.

3 cups cooked spaghetti squash	**2 tablespoons snipped fresh chives**
3 tablespoons oil	**or 1 tablespoon dried**
1 tablespoon vinegar	**½-¾ cup minced celery hearts**
Salt	**with leaves**

Combine squash, oil, vinegar, and ¼ teaspoon salt. Add chives and celery and mix well. Let sit a few hours before serving. Taste—you may want more salt.   *Serves 5-6.*

Other Ideas for Winter Squash

- ° Cook winter squash with apples for soup. Use your imagination in seasoning squash soup, which is beautiful puréed with cream—try thyme or rosemary, or such spices as nutmeg, cinnamon, allspice, mace, or add curry or chili powder.
- ° Immature winter squash, especially Hubbard, are delicious sliced, brushed with oil, and grilled over coals.
- ° To cook squash quickly, grate it and stir-fry.
- ° Slice peeled squash very thin (or grate) and layer in a casserole with cinnamon-flavored cream. Dot with butter and bake at 350° F. for 1½ hours.
- ° Maple syrup is wonderful with winter squash. Use it when baking acorn squash, or top squash pie with whipped cream into which you have lightly folded ribbons of maple syrup.
- ° The Japanese use winter squash imaginatively for its color— for instance, they serve cubes of orange squash on a plate with bright green spinach and shrimp. Consider using squash as a colorful accent in the menu.
- ° For a meal in a shell, rub squash halves generously with butter and bake for 40 minutes at 350° F. Remove from oven

and mix the liquid that has accumulated in squash cavities with diced cooked pork, diced tart apples, some bread crumbs, sunflower seeds (if you like), and sage. Season to taste, fill cavities, cover loosely with foil, and bake 30 more minutes.

∘ Squash blossoms along with their tender stems can be deep-fried or sautéed. Pick male blossoms—ones without a green ball at the base.

∘ Peel and slice squash, top with sliced apples, peaches, and apricots, pour on a syrup of melted butter, brown sugar, and curry powder, and bake at 350° F. for about 40 minutes.

∘ Use puréed squash instead of applesauce in applesauce cake.

∘ To roast squash seeds let them dry out a bit, then oil them lightly, place on a baking tray, and roast in a 375° oven for 10–20 minutes, until lightly browned.

∘ Substitute grated winter squash for carrots in Carrot Drop Cookies, or use instead of zucchini in Golden Zucchini Tea Cake.

Sweet potatoes are a tropical American vegetable taken to Spain by the conquistadors. Unlike most of the other vegetable imports, they became popular right away in heavily spiced and sweetened pies. I grew them for the first time in the summer of 1981. The plants produced a beautiful green mat, but the tubers were long and thin, as my soil was too heavy.

Sweet potatoes belong to the morning glory family, and there are two types. One has a dry texture, yellow skin, and pale flesh; the other has a moist texture and vivid orange flesh. Moist-fleshed sweet potatoes are often called yams, which they are not. True yams are a tropical plant botanically unrelated to the sweet potato, though similar in appearance. Some of the early cooks in this country called the moister sweet potatoes "yams" because they resembled their native African food *nyami*, which grows much larger, does not contain the abundant vitamin A of the sweet potato, and is rarely found in the United States.

Sweet potatoes need a long, warm growing season—some 150 days. They are grown from young plants called "slips," which are usually purchased, since a hot bed is required to grow them from tubers. The slips have very few roots, so it is important to use Transplantone when they are set out in the garden as soon as the soil has warmed up. Plant them at least a foot apart in a mounded row over deeply dug soil. They will produce better tubers in a light, pliable soil than a heavy one. They need a lot of water just after planting, though not after the plants have grown awhile. Harvest them when the leaves begin to wither and before a heavy frost. A light frost will not injure the tubers.

After harvesting, the tubers should be kept in a moist, warm atmosphere while the skins cure. When the skins have become firm, they then are stored in a dry spot at a temperature around 55° F. They do not keep nearly as well as white potatoes.

My favorite way to serve sweet potatoes is to bake them. I scrub them well first, as I like to eat the skins, and bake them at 400° F. for up to an hour, or until they feel tender when squeezed. They can also be boiled in their jackets for 20–30 minutes, then peeled and mashed. If you must peel them before cooking, drop them in cold water to prevent discoloring until ready to cook.

Other Ideas for Sweet Potatoes

○ Good seasonings for sweet potatoes are butter, nutmeg, orange rind, or a topping of marshmallows browned under the broiler. They also combine well with ham and sausage, maple syrup, apples, raisins, and nuts. Try baked sweet potatoes with simply a drizzle of warm butter and a splash of sherry.

- In Louisiana, grated raw sweet potatoes are combined with diced apples, pecans, raisins, celery, and enough mayonnaise to bind the salad.
- For moist sweet-potato biscuits, perfect with smoky ham, sift together 1½ cups flour, 1½ teaspoons baking powder, and ½ teaspoon salt. Cut in 3 tablespoons butter and ½ cup cold mashed sweet potatoes. Moisten with about 6 tablespoons milk to make a soft dough, knead just until smooth, and cut out small biscuits ½ inch thick. Bake at 450° F. until browned.
- Braise thick slices of parboiled sweet potatoes with pork chops.
- For grilled sweet potatoes, cook potatoes in jackets until barely tender, peel, and cut thick lengthwise slices. Brush with butter and grill over hot coals or under broiler, turning several times, until lightly browned.
- To fry sweet potatoes, first boil them in their skins for 10 minutes. Peel, slice, and fry in plenty of oil until lightly browned. Or cook raw slices as tempura.
- Make scalloped sweet potatoes by layering them, boiled and sliced, with thinly sliced apples and/or oranges. Sprinkle layers with brown sugar, dot with butter, and bake, covered, for 30 minutes at 350° F. Uncover. Bake 30 more minutes.
- Add crushed pineapple and chopped pecans to mashed sweet potatoes. Or pour molasses and melted butter on top and bake in a 400° oven until brown on top.
- A lovely garnish for the Thanksgiving turkey or ham: Cut orange slices, remove centers, and boil slices until tender in a light syrup. Deep-fry long, narrow French fries of sweet potatoes and insert them like sheaves in the orange rings.
- Substitute puréed sweet potatoes for pumpkin in your favorite pie recipe.
- The Japanese make elegant "chestnuts" from sweet potatoes. To create this sweet confection, steam 3 peeled sweet potatoes until tender, then purée. Make a syrup of 2 cups sugar and 2 cups water. Blend cooled potatoes and syrup with 3 egg yolks in double boiler and stir constantly over heat until fluffy. Cool, then pat purée into chestnut-size balls. Place one in center of a cotton napkin, gather up ends, and wring to release liquid. Unwrap to reveal a molded "chestnut."

Late
Turnips
and
Rutabagas

I have already written about white turnips for the early garden. As they are quick growers, they can also be planted in late summer for fall use. In America, turnip greens are associated with the South, as the plants will grow there through the winter.

Both rutabagas and turnips are members of the cabbage family, but the rutabaga has a particularly confusing nomenclature. Depending on where you live, it is called yellow turnip, Canadian turnip, Russian turnip, Swedish turnip, swede, or neeps. Rutabagas take three months to mature and are planted for a fall crop. They resemble pale yellow cannonballs, often with the aboveground portion a dark reddish purple, and their flesh is more yellow than that of turnips, especially when cooked. They are much larger than early white turnips, and when old can get woody.

Rutabaga seeds are sown directly in the garden and usually will germinate in a week. As the young plants grow, some can be pulled out and used so as to give the rest room to develop roots. The roots can grow quite large, so the plants should be about five inches apart. Use the young plants for greens—unlike turnip greens, the leaves of older rutabaga plants are too coarse and bitter for most people's taste. The mature roots can be stored in a cool cellar to use all winter.

In general, rutabagas can be used in any way you would cook turnips (see ideas where turnips are discussed), but they have a denser texture and require longer cooking—30–40 minutes' boiling or steaming. They also have a sweeter and more assertive flavor.

◦ *Mashed Rutabagas (A Traditional Thanksgiving Dish)*

Peel and boil rutabagas until tender. Also boil 1 potato in its skin for every 2 rutabagas (this can be done in the same pot, but potatoes will cook faster). Peel and mash potatoes while hot. Mash the rutabagas and mix the two. Season with butter and salt.

Other Ideas for Rutabagas

- ◦ I think rutabagas go best as a side vegetable with turkey and in beef stew.
- ◦ Peel and grate raw rutabagas and dress with vinaigrette or mayonnaise well flavored with herbs.
- ◦ For New England rutabaga salad, combine grated young rutabaga, celery, scallions, and torn romaine leaves. Dress with a mixture of oil, vinegar, chopped basil, and a little sugar and dry mustard.
- ◦ Make rutabaga soufflé with mashed rutabagas and grated Colby cheese.
- ◦ Finnish rutabaga pudding is made by mashing rutabagas, adding cream, butter, sugar, and nutmeg, and baking at 375° F. until top is browned. You might also use mace or ginger, and add an egg and bread crumbs. This can also be used as filling for a pie.
- ◦ Make a duck stew with rutabagas and plenty of thyme for seasoning.
- ◦ Mash rutabagas with cooked tart apples and season with a little sugar and cardamom.
- ◦ For a rich flavor, wrap scrubbed rutabagas in foil and roast in hot ashes until they feel tender when squeezed—try doing it in the fireplace.
- ◦ In the "olden days," rutabagas were often the first vegetable planted in newly broken soil on the plains, and the pioneers served rutabaga pies. I imagine they were made the same way as pumpkin pie, but I would think they would need less spice.

Stocking
the larder.

In Palestine the pantry in our home was a fascinating room. In it were stored all the supplies from Scotland, which were ordered only once a year. What fun it was to unpack those crates and discover that some special hard candies, such as black-and-white strong peppermint-flavored bull's eyes, had been included! Cinnamon sticks and raisins were also stored in the pantry and secretly taken by us children when the door was left unlocked.

In Connecticut my grandfather built a dugout cellar in the side of the hill in which to store apples, cabbages wrapped in newspapers, and barrels of root crops. When the temperature got to zero, he lit a small kerosene stove. Eggs, when plentiful, were stored in the cellar in "water glass," a gelatinous white mass that kept oxygen from the eggs to prevent spoilage. The surplus vegetables, such as corn and green beans, were packed in jars, processed in a huge oval canning pot that covered two burners on the stove, and boiled for ages, heating up the summer kitchen. We children had to help in preparing the vegetables, and we invented games or found some form of competition to make the job fun. Fruits were made into jams or sauces. There were times when we were snowbound, so this winter stock was very useful.

Thanks to the advent of the freezer, I do not have to go

through all those lengthy procedures to store the surplus from my garden. But I still can tomatoes, applesauce, and peaches. I know that some people freeze tomatoes, but I prefer to save my freezer space for green and nonacid vegetables. If you like to can, consult a current book on the subject, and be careful when canning tomatoes to add lemon juice or citric acid to low-acid tomatoes.

Pickles

Making pickles is lots of fun, and oh, how tantalizing the kitchen smells in the process! It's a great way to make use of appropriate vegetables when you do not choose to can or freeze them. And what a satisfaction it is to have a well-stocked shelf of assorted pickles to draw on when you are about to serve a meal and feel that something is lacking to give it zip—especially when serving cold meats.

One day in midwinter I had to serve an informal lunch to an unknown number of guests following a service that I also attended. I served cold meats, hot baked beans, and assorted pickles—dilled whole string beans, red beets (sour), Golden Beet Pickle (sweet), and Jerusalem Artichoke Relish. By adding color and interest to the lunch, these pickles made an ordinary meal special.

In the old days, large quantities of pickles were made at one time, as this was the only safe way most surplus vegetables could be processed for winter. The recipes called for bushels or quarts of vegetables and gallons of brine. I make a half gallon of pickle brine, using what is needed for the quantity of vegetables to be pickled and saving the rest for use later. It's easy to do two pints of cucumbers or other pickles this way.

Many recipes—old ones especially—call for sprinkling salt on layers of cucumbers and leaving them overnight. Don't make the mistake I have of putting too much salt on or leaving them too long—the result is limp, pale pickles. Always use plain salt, not iodized, and white vinegar if you want to preserve color.

I have also made the mistake of packing my jars too tight before adding the pickle brine. When I wondered why my pepper relish had no flavor, I realized that the flavor was in the brine, and I had not put enough in the jar to give the peppers the desired taste. You should be able to stir the vegetables around in the brine in the jars.

○ *Mother's Bread-and-Butter Pickles from Connecticut*

These pickles spread over bread and butter were a treat for my mother when she visited her grandmother on the family farm in Connecticut. They are my favorite to serve with any meat and also to add to a green salad to give it a surprise touch when I have no tomatoes or aspic to use. I also use Golden Beet Pickle for this purpose; see recipe.

2 dozen unpeeled cucumbers no more than 1½ inches in diameter	5 cups sugar
	1½ teaspoons turmeric
8 medium onions	½ teaspoon ground cloves
½ cup salt	2 teaspoons mustard seed
5 cups white vinegar	1 teaspoon celery seed

Thinly slice the cucumbers and onions and put in a bowl with the salt sprinkled between the layers. Add 1 cup water and let stand for about 3 hours. Strain.

Cook the remaining ingredients over low heat, stirring until sugar dissolves. Add the cucumber and onion. Heat very slowly until hot but not quite boiling. Put in sterilized jars while hot and seal at once. *Makes about 12 pints*

○ *Jerusalem Artichoke Relish*

4 quarts Jerusalem artichokes	4 tablespoons dry mustard
1 quart onions	2 tablespoons grated fresh ginger
3 large sweet red peppers	1 tablespoon turmeric
1½ cups salt	2 tablespoons celery seed
2 quarts vinegar	4 cups sugar
1 cup flour	

Wash and scrub the Jerusalem artichokes with a plastic scouring pad. Put artichokes, onions, and peppers through the grater of a food processor, or grate on the wide opening of a hand grater. Cover with 1 gallon of water and the salt. Let stand for 24 hours, then drain well.

Make a soft paste of 1 cup vinegar and the remaining ingredients. Heat the rest of the vinegar, add the paste, and cook until vinegar thickens, stirring constantly. Add the drained vegetables and bring to a boil. Put in hot sterilized jars and seal as you fill each one.

Makes about 12 pints

○ *Apple and Cantaloupe Chutney*

Very often wildlife will test a cantaloupe in your garden just before it is quite ripe. Or you will buy a melon and cut into it only to discover it has little flavor. If this happens, make chutney.

1½ cups chopped peeled apples
1½ cups chopped semiripe
  cantaloupe
1 cup chopped onion
½ cup seedless raisins
1 cup firmly packed brown sugar
1 cup white or cider vinegar
2 tablespoons peeled, chopped
  fresh red hot pepper

1 medium-size red sweet pepper,
  peeled and chopped
1 really small clove garlic,
  chopped fine
1 teaspoon ground ginger
½ teaspoon salt
⅓ teaspoon ground cinnamon

Mix all together and bring to a boil, stirring now and then. Simmer for 2–3 hours until it has reduced to half its original volume. Put in sterilized jars while hot and seal.

Makes 4 half-pints

Jams and Jellies

These are nice to have on hand and, with commercial pectins, so much quicker to make than in the old days. I find it more satisfactory to seal my jam and jellies with metal caps rather than paraffin.

° Mint-Apple Jelly

Serve this jelly with hot or cold lamb.

2 cups tightly packed fresh mint leaves	¼ cup white vinegar
3 cups unsweetened apple juice	1 packet Sure-Jell
	4 cups sugar

Put the mint leaves, apple juice, and vinegar in a pot and slowly bring to a boil. Remove from heat. Steep for 15 minutes. Strain.

Put 3 cups of the mint infusion in a 4-quart pot and add the packet of Sure-Jell. Mix well and bring to a rolling boil. Add the sugar and bring back to a rolling boil for 1 minute, stirring all the time. (It is safer to boil for a little longer than a shorter time.)

Remove from heat and skim off foam. Fill sterilized jars and seal with canning jar lids or hot paraffin, following package instructions. *Makes about 4 cups.*

° Rhubarb Marmalade

1 lemon	3¼ cups sugar
1 orange	1 tablespoon finely chopped
1¾ pounds rhubarb, chopped fine	candied ginger (optional)
⅓ cup golden raisins	

Squeeze the lemon and orange and reserve the juice. Remove white pulp and finely chop the rinds. Combine with rhubarb, raisins, sugar, and ginger (if you like) and let sit overnight.

Add the juice of the lemon and orange to the rhubarb and cook until thick, stirring frequently. Put in sterilized jelly jars while hot and seal with canning lids or hot paraffin, according to package directions. *Makes 4 cups.*

° Wineberry Jelly

Wineberries have become wild in eastern Pennsylvania. They were introduced by early settlers who hoped to cultivate them for wine, but they will grow only in partial shade at the edge of woods. They are similar in shape to a raspberry, and just as fragile, but are a shiny clear bright red when almost ripe and turn more raspberry-colored when fully ripe. Here in Pennsylvania they are ripe the second or third week of July.

I love freshly picked wineberries for breakfast. They are the most refreshing berry I know of, and they make a most delicious tart jelly. Any wineberry juice left over from making jelly is excellent added to strawberry or raspberry gelatin in place of some of the water. Add the juice to 7-Up for a refreshing drink.

3 quarts wineberries
1 teaspoon finely grated lemon rind

1 box Sure-Jell
5½ cups sugar

Put wineberries in a stainless-steel or agate pot. Crush them and bring them to a boil, stirring occasionally, then let them simmer for at least 15 minutes. Pour the berries into a jelly bag, hang it over a bowl, and let juice drip through. (I find hot juice goes through a bag more quickly than cold juice.) Let it drip for at least 2 hours. Don't squeeze it tightly to get the last drop—just apply light pressure.

Measure 4 cups juice and pour it into a large stainless-steel or agate pot that holds at least 5 quarts. At one point in the process the contents will foam way up in the pot. Add the lemon rind and Sure-Jell. Stir it well and bring to a bubbling boil over high heat, stirring now and then. Add the sugar and bring to a full rolling boil. This is when everything in the pot rises and you think you'll have a mess on the stove, but with a large pot you will be okay. The contents should stay up in the pot while you stir it for 1 minute—don't skimp on the time, a little more won't hurt. Remove from stove and scoop off any scum. Fill warmed sterilized jars to within ¼ inch of top. Seal with canning lids or hot paraffin, according to package directions. *Makes 6 cups.*

Freezing Vegetables

I find it best to make several plantings of those vegetables I wish to freeze rather than to make one large planting. One never knows what might come up in your daily life requiring time just when the crop is at its peak for freezing.

I use an agate spaghetti cooker for blanching vegetables (the same pot I use for making jelly), a large bowl in which a colander can sit with its rim above the bowl's rim for cooling the blanched vegetable, and a white all-cotton terry bath towel for drying the vegetables before packaging. I cool the vegetables in running cold water and pat or shake them in the towel to dry.

Blanching is done for two reasons: to kill fungi that may be on the vegetable and to stop enzyme action. So follow directions on time for blanching on a freezing chart. It is important to bring the water back to the boiling point as quickly as possible, so blanch no more than three or four cups of vegetables at a time. Do not overdo the blanching time, and cool the vegetables quickly or they will be mushy.

Choose freezer bags of a size that suits your family's needs. Fill bags only to within 2½ inches of the top. Twist the top and, with the other hand, press the air out. Then twist again, turn top over, and tie. It's the same way I tie a balloon. Now you can form the bag into a flat block with straight sides, which will pack neatly in the freezer. There is nothing more annoying than to have bulky, rounded frozen packages come tumbling out of the freezer when you open the door.

Labeling is important. You think you will be able to see through bags, but after a few months you won't be able to tell what is in them because of frost.

My freezer is an upright one, and I have made a chart on the door to show where I have put each kind of vegetable. There are some that I do only in small quantities, such as okra, peppers, and herbs. To keep these from getting lost, I use a half-gallon milk carton, putting the small packets in it—one carton for each kind—and marking it with a wax crayon.

It's not necessary to spend a fortune on freezing equipment. Milk cartons, quart size, may be used for storing stock. I staple the carton closed and run freezer tape over the edge. They pack better than round containers. But you can also use cottage cheese containers for smaller amounts or for fruits in syrup or applesauce. Leave an inch at the top for expansion.

Freezing Berries

Wash strawberries and blueberries and dry them on a towel. Do not wash raspberries—have clean hands and use clean containers when you pick.

Put wax paper on a cookie sheet and spread the berries out on it in one layer. Look them over for any moldy spots. Put the cookie sheet in the freezer. The berries should be frozen in thirty minutes. Take your containers to the freezer and fill them with the frozen berries. Make flat packages so they will thaw quickly in the package when you wish to use them. Do not add sugar; you can do it later.

I also freeze some half pints of raspberry juice to use in making sauces or for my blueberry pie. Boil the berries and then strain them. The juice does not have to be clear as it does for a jelly, so you can squeeze the fruit to extract all the juice possible.

Drying and Freezing Herbs

I use my small appliance oven to dry a few herbs quickly. Clean the herb leaves if necessary and pat them dry. Put two layers of aluminum foil over the oven rack and let it be a bit crinkled. Spread the leaves on this in one layer (a little overlapping is okay). Put the rack in the center of the oven and turn the heat on the lowest temperature possible. Leave it on overnight; in the morning the herbs should be dry enough to crumble. This works very well for basil, dill, and parsley, particularly as it helps keep their color. You can, of course, dry them similarly in the stove oven.

The firmer-leafed herbs, such as thyme, savory, and sage do not have to be kept green, and can be dried more slowly. Pick long stems of them just before they are about to bloom and wash them if necessary. Make small bunches and place each one in a plastic or brown paper bag that has holes in it so that the stems are at the

> ### Herb-Flavored Stock
>
> I save all my chicken bones and make stock. In the fall, I season a batch quite heavily with fresh rosemary and another with fresh tarragon, strain and cool it, and freeze it in ice-cube trays. Then I remove it from the trays and store the cubes of concentrated herb-flavored stock in bags in the freezer (labeled, of course), so it's easy to pop a cube into winter soups or dishes to get the desired herb flavor. This gives me variety with the same basic stock, and fresh tarragon and rosemary flavors are far superior to dried.

bottom of the bag. Tie the bag around the stems and hang in a dry place, such as in the attic or over the furnace or hot-water heater. Keep the bags open so the dry warm air can enter. When dry, remove the leaves and store them in bottles in a dark place to preserve their color. Herbs lose a lot of their flavor in a year, so do not dry more than you can use in that time.

Most herbs are dried, but some green ones, such as parsley, chives, and basil, give a fresher flavor when frozen for winter use. I spread washed and towel-dried leaves on a cookie sheet, which I place on a freezer shelf overnight. Then I quickly put a few of the leaves in small freezer or sandwich bags. I put the bags in cut-off milk cartons—labeled—so I can quickly find and take out a packet from the freezer for use as wanted.

○ Borscht Concentrate for the Freezer

With this concentrate on hand you can prepare a quick borscht any time of the year.

2 cups shredded beets	½ cup shredded celery (optional)
1 cup shredded onion	2 cups tomato juice
1 cup shredded carrot	1½ teaspoons salt
1 cup shredded red cabbage	

Mix all in a pot and bring just to a boil. Cool and fill pint containers and freeze. When you want to serve this soup, add the vegetables to

3 cups of either beef or chicken stock, and add a bay leaf and a few sprigs of fresh thyme while it is cooking. Simmer covered for 45 minutes. Remove herbs before serving. It may need more salt. Put sour cream on top of each serving. *Serves 6.*

° Frozen Cranberry Relish

I particularly like to have refreshing raw cranberry relish to serve with cold fowl in summer. As cranberries are not available in the summer, I make this in November or December and put it in the freezer.

1 orange with medium-thick rind
1 medium-size lemon
1 pound fresh cranberries, checked
   over and washed

2 medium-size red apples
¾ cup sugar or ⅔ cup honey

Cut the orange and lemon into narrow sections and put through the fine disk of a meat grinder. Change grinder disk to a coarser cut and put cranberries and apples through grinder. Add sugar or honey to mixture, stir, cover, and let sit in bowl in cool place overnight. Stir again, taste to see if you want it sweeter, and add more sugar or honey if you like. Fill containers to 1 inch from the rim and freeze. *Makes 3 6-ounce containers.*

Being a gardener, I do prefer to be outside rather than in the kitchen. The freshness of the air, the fragrance of flowers, vegetables, and herbs as I work among them carry my mind away from critical thoughts and world problems to creative ideas. The brown thrasher and the mockingbird challenge my right to their berries, and I enjoy their delightful protest and laugh. It reminds me of a song my family sang at family prayers.

> There's a solemn little bird of sober hue
> To-whit, to-whit, to who:
> And every single second of the time he does
> Just what God means him to.
> Hear his solemn little message to you,
> My dears—"To-whit, to-whit, to who!
> Just what God means me to be, I AM!
> To-whit—to whoo! Are you?

This is true of everything growing outdoors if we give it a chance.

So the desserts I make are those that can be put together quickly and on the spur of the moment. I use prepared mixes, and I make graham-cracker-crust pies, which do not require all that cutting in of shortening and rolling out of dough. I guess I really am lazy—I try to think of the easiest way to get things done indoors in the shortest time so I can get back out to the garden.

With rhubarb, berries, and melon, I am able to get something from the garden for desserts from spring to frost. Also, if my crop has been good and the wildlife not too piggish, I'll have fruits in the freezer.

When I plan a rather filling dinner of roast and potatoes and other vegetables, I serve a light dessert, such as a mixture of fruits from the garden with cookies. When the main course is one of my concoctions using leftovers, I bake a favorite dessert, such as a cobbler or cake, using fruit.

Rhubarb

This vegetable is discussed on pages 59–61, and I've given a recipe there for stewed rhubarb as well as other ideas for using rhubarb.

∘ *Rhubarb Cake*

Serve this tartlike cake with vanilla ice cream or ice milk.

1¼ cups biscuit mix (or your own baking-powder-biscuit recipe)	2 tablespoons cornstarch
1 egg	4 cups chopped raw rhubarb
1 cup plus 2 tablespoons sugar	1½ tablespoons flour
7 tablespoons butter, softened	¼ teaspoon ground ginger

Measure biscuit mix into a bowl and add egg, 2 tablespoons sugar, and 4 tablespoons butter. Blend together into a dough. Press dough into an ungreased 11x7-inch pan until bottom is covered.

Mix ½ cup sugar with cornstarch, stir into the rhubarb, spread mixture over the dough, and press down. Sprinkle any sugar and cornstarch remaining in the bowl over the rhubarb.

For the topping, mix ½ cup sugar, flour, ginger, and 3 tablespoons butter until crumbly and sprinkle over rhubarb.

Bake in a 350° oven for 45 minutes. Remove cake from the oven, run a knife around the edge of the pan, and cool on a rack.

Serves 6-8

○ Rhubarb-Pineapple Sauce

This sauce, from a rhubarb grower, Elizabeth V. Shelley, is excellent on cheesecake, ice cream, or plain cake.

9 stalks rhubarb, 12 inches long, cut in 1-inch pieces
20-ounce can crushed pineapple

3-ounce packet strawberry-flavored gelatin

Put rhubarb in a pot (not aluminum) and empty can of pineapple, including juice, on top. Bring slowly to a boil over medium heat, and cook until tender. Add strawberry gelatin and stir it in well. Cool. *Makes about 4 cups.*

Strawberries

Strawberries come after the rhubarb harvest. Let them ripen on the plants unless rain is predicted, when berries with a white tip may be ripened in the house. Do not wash them until ready to use. I think refrigerating berries takes away some of their sweetness. After picking, I spread the berries out on a tray covered with wax paper and place it by a cool window (not in the sun). Wash the berries just before serving and dry on a paper towel.

○ Strawberry Sauce

For a sauce for ice cream or pudding, I prefer to chop strawberries rather than mash them because the sauce looks better. One-quarter cup sugar to 1 cup chopped fruit is plenty sweet.

To serve over cheesecake, the berry juice needs a little thickening: For 3 cups sauce, or 6 servings, cook 1 cup finely chopped strawberries in ½ cup water for 3 minutes. Stir in ¾ cup sugar and 2 tablespoons cornstarch mixed in ¼ cup water. Cook until clear, then cool a little. Add 2 cups fresh berries, cut in half if small, in quarters if large.

° Strawberry Sherbet

Garnish this sherbet with whole berries when serving, if you wish.

1 quart strawberries	1½ cups buttermilk
¾ cup sugar	2 tablespoons lemon juice
1 envelope unflavored gelatin	

Clean and slice strawberries, then mash them with ¼ cup sugar. Let stand for 10 minutes. Strain off ½ cup of the strawberry juice, stir in gelatin, and dissolve in a pot over hot water. Add the crushed berries, buttermilk, ½ cup sugar, and lemon juice. Stir well to dissolve all sugar. Freeze until mushy. Then beat in a mixing bowl until smooth. Return to refrigerator tray and freeze until firm.

Makes about 1 quart.

° Strawberry or Raspberry New England Shortcake

Peaches can be used instead of berries in this recipe.

2 cups flour, sifted	½ cup butter or shortening
2½ teaspoons baking powder	¾ cup milk
½ teaspoon salt	6 cups fresh strawberries or
1½ cups plus 2 tablespoons sugar	raspberries

Sift together flour, baking powder, salt, and 2 tablespoons sugar. Work in the butter or shortening, and add the milk. Divide and roll out each half to the size of a baking dish approximately 9 inches in diameter. Put one half in, brush lightly with oil, and place other half on top. Bake in a 375° oven for 30–45 minutes.

Wash and dry the berries. Slice or halve strawberries if you like. Add 1½ cups sugar and let stand in a cool place for about 15 minutes. Turn the fruit over now and then.

When biscuit is baked, cool until not too hot to handle. Separate the two layers with a knife. Place the bottom layer on a serving dish. Put half the berries over it while it is a little warm so that the juice will penetrate. Put top layer on and cover with the rest of the fruit. The fruit should go on at least 10 minutes before serving.

Serves 6–8

Raspberries

My guests exclaim over being served fresh raspberries, as they are so expensive and not often found in the market. Breeders seem to be trying to develop raspberries that will hold their shape and not crumble, but I find weather has a good deal to do with how the berries hold up after picking. They are the only berry that produces a good two-season crop. But to get two seasons you must plant the so-called everbearing varieties. This is a misnomer—actually they bear only in late June or early July and again in September and October. One mild fall season I was still picking in November. For a good fall crop the bushes must get water in August. My fall crop is often better than the summer one.

The structure of raspberries is so delicate they should be picked into boxes no larger than a pint. I use empty cottage-cheese containers. Since it takes two hands to pick berries. I make a hanging container with a paper paint bucket and string and hang it around my neck. The cottage-cheese box goes into this. Raspberries are the only berries I refrigerate because they mold so quickly in our humidity. If you are not using the berries until the next day, first thing in the morning dump them into another container. This separates the berries and helps to stave off molding.

Since my husband objected to raspberry seeds, I sieve the berries, using a stainless-steel strainer, after heating them until they become juicy. I use this juice to make sauce for ice cream, custards, puddings, or cheesecake. When we have guests, I serve both fresh berries and sauce.

○ Whipped Raspberry Gelatin

1 envelope unflavored gelatin	2 tablespoons sugar
2 cups raspberry juice	

Shake the gelatin over 1 cup juice and let stand 5 minutes. Bring the other cup of juice to a boil and pour over the gelatin and juice. Add the sugar and mix well to be sure it is all dissolved.

Put in a bowl that will hold at least twice the volume and refrigerate. When gelatin has started to set but is not firm, beat with an electric beater at high speed for at least 3 minutes. The volume will increase dramatically. Return to the refrigerator for at least 30 minutes before serving. *Serves 6-7*

Blueberries

These are the next berries to ripen after raspberries. In order to have fully ripened, sweet, flavorful berries, I grow mine in a wire house to keep the birds out. For picking, I use the same paint bucket hung around my neck that I use for raspberries. Blueberries turn blue long before they are sweet. Wait until the white bloom on them disappears—they then roll off the bush into your hand when your fingers brush over them—and you will have the true blueberry flavor. And don't refrigerate them. Refrigerated blueberries become sour and flavorless. Keep them in ventilated containers out of reach of too friendly field mice. They love them.

○ *Blueberry Pie*

Make graham-cracker crust as directed on the cracker package, but add 1 tablespoon water. Spread and press into a 9-inch pie plate and well up the sides. Bake for 8 minutes in a 375° oven. If the sides slip down in baking, a little pressure with the spoon while crust is still warm will push them up again.

1 graham-cracker crust	1 quart blueberries
3 tablespoons cornstarch	¾ cup sugar
1 cup raspberry juice from 1 pint raspberries	Powdered sugar or whipped cream (optional)

Mix cornstarch with raspberry juice in a double boiler or heavy stainless-steel pan. Add 1 cup blueberries and the sugar. Cook, stirring frequently, until the color is clear, not chalky, about 20 minutes. Add 2 cups blueberries and cook just until berries are warmed through and still have their shape. Taste for sweetness. More sugar may be desired. Pour into the pie shell. Place the remaining cup of berries in a design over the top. Chill and serve. You may shake powdered sugar over the top just before serving, or serve with whipped cream.

° *Blueberry Crumb Pudding*

1 cup zwieback crumbs (8-10
  slices)
½ teaspoon cinnamon
¼ cup sugar
½ teaspoon grated lemon rind
3 tablespoons butter, melted

2 cups blueberries
½ cup raspberry juice, or juice
  from canned fruit (not syrup)
Whipped cream or vanilla ice
  cream

Combine the crumbs, cinnamon, sugar, and lemon rind. Mix in butter thoroughly. Place 1 cup of the blueberries in a buttered 1-quart casserole. Cover with half the crumb mixture. Add remaining blueberries and top with remaining crumbs. Pour the fruit juice over the dish. Press down with a spoon. Bake in a preheated 350° oven for 30 minutes. Serve at room temperature with whipped cream, or hot with ice cream. *Serves 4-5*

Variations: Vanilla wafers mixed with shredded wheat and made into crumbs may be used in place of zwieback. If frozen berries are used, add a little extra sugar. Do not thaw the berries, but cook the pudding another 15 minutes, or a total of 45 minutes.

° *Blueberry Sauce*

Blueberries make a delicious sauce for ice cream or cheesecake. A little fresh-grated lemon rind gives more character to the flavor. I use cornstarch or tapioca flour when making fruit sauces because they do not dull the bright color of fruits as flour does.

1 teaspoon cornstarch or tapioca
  flour
½ cup water

¼ cup sugar
¼ teaspoon grated lemon rind
1½ cups blueberries

Mix cornstarch or tapioca flour and water in the top of a double boiler or heavy pan. Let it sit for 10 minutes. Add the sugar and lemon rind and cook, stirring frequently. When the syrup has lost its chalky look, add the berries and cook only until the juice comes out of them. Stir frequently. You may like more sugar. *Makes 2 cups.*

Quick Fresh Fruit Sauce

Using wine with fresh fruits is a way to produce a quick shortcake when you don't have enough fruit to mash to produce juice. Pour ½ cup pink or white Catawba wine over 1 cup sliced strawberries, peaches, or raspberries. Add 2 tablespoons sugar and let sit 10 minutes or so. Serve over squares of a light cake or split hot biscuits.

Melons

Gardeners take great pride in their melons—they are indeed a luxury when allowed to ripen on the vine. So much more sugar develops in vine-ripened fruit than in the commercial melons picked half green.

Melons need hot weather to grow well. I prefer to plant seed directly in the garden and protect the seed and seedlings with Hotkaps. The seeds are usually planted in hills about a foot across, and three plants are selected to grow in each hill. Where the growing season is short, they can be started indoors in six-inch peat pots. The plants do not have a lot of fibrous roots, so when they are put in the garden, soak the soil and cut the pot away from the roots. Set the plants three or four feet apart in a row and water well. Melon vines produce male and female blossoms, and only the latter become melons. The female blossom has a green knob at the base of the yellow petal tube.

When selecting melons for your garden, do pay attention to the number of days it takes to get a ripe melon. Cantaloupes are earlier than Crenshaws, honey dews, casabas, or watermelons. Ordinary watermelons take a great deal of room and spread all over a garden, but they are hardier plants. A bush type has been developed which has small fruits but not as many as the vine varieties.

At the end of the blueberry season the cantaloupes are ripening. When I notice a melon getting large, I place under it an inverted aluminum pie plate with punched drainage holes. This protects the fruit from active creatures in the soil.

To tell when a cantaloupe is ripe, look at the fruit where its stem is attached to the vine. Drops of sap appear first and then a small crack. When there is a real crack at the stem, the melon is ripe and will separate from the vine with only a small twist. If there is any resistance, let the melon stay another day. I leave my melons in a cool room until ready to prepare them. After cutting and removing the seeds, I refrigerate the pieces for a short time.

When serving melons for dessert at a party, I place a flower in the center—nasturtiums if I have some, as they are edible.

Melon seeds are edible. Dry them, put them in a fry pan, and pour some salted water over them. Stir over heat until the water has gone, then start nibbling.

Watermelon is a dramatic fruit that now comes in all sizes with or without seeds. To determine ripeness, I look for a hint of yellowing on the underside and brown streaks on the stem. Knocking a melon will also tell you if you have a ripe one. If there is only a thud, it's not ripe; if there's a bit of resonance, it's ripe. If it really sounds hollow, it's overripe.

I have kept picked watermelons and Crenshaw melons in a cool place and they were edible in November. These were melons that were picked before a frost was expected and not quite ripe.

Other Desserts from the Garden

○ Fruit Cobblers

Cobblers are easy to make—there is no rolling of dough, and you can use fresh, frozen, or canned fruit. Cobblers should be served warm in the dish they are baked in. They are especially good with vanilla ice cream on the side.

Cobblers have more juice than pies, and a little thickening is needed. For 4 cups fresh berries, use 2 tablespoons cornstarch mixed in ¼ cup water or any fruit juice. Add 1 cup sugar.

For 3 cups cooked or frozen fruit, use 2 tablespoons quick-cooking tapioca. Mix them and let stand for 15 minutes. If fruit has not been sweetened, add 1 cup sugar. To blueberries, add 2 tablespoons lemon juice or 1 tablespoon juice and ⅓ tablespoon grated rind. To blackberries, add 1 tablespoon grated lemon rind.

Peel fresh peaches or plums, remove seeds, then use the same quantities of fruit, cornstarch, and sugar as for fresh berries. To peaches, add ¼ teaspoon almond flavoring, 1 tablespoon grated orange rind, and ½ teaspoon cinnamon (optional). If plums are sour, use ¼ cup more sugar and ½ teaspoon cinnamon.

Some good combinations of fruits are blueberries and raspberries; ⅔ cup blueberries and ⅓ cup crushed pineapple; peaches and apricots; strawberries and rhubarb.

All too often bugs and birds force me to pick fruit before it has ripened to its full flavor. To compensate for this, I use jam of a like fruit as well as marmalade in place of some of the sugar. I watch for sales and keep peach and apricot jam and marmalade of a less expensive brand on hand just for this use. I like to use the apricot jam with peaches. Peach jam can be used with blackberries as well as peaches. Marmalade goes well with anything.

Put the fruit mixture in a flameproof 9-inch dish that's at least 2 inches deep. Dot with 2 tablespoons butter. Heat the fruit, covered, until juice is boiling. Meanwhile make the following dough for topping (or use recipe for shortcake, page 203, or your own baking-powder-biscuit recipe).

1½ cups biscuit mix	1 medium egg
3 tablespoons oil or melted butter	½ cup milk
2 tablespoons sugar	

Combine biscuit mix with rest of ingredients. Drop the dough by teaspoonfuls over the hot fruit, leaving ¾ inch between the drops. You may not need to use all the dough—bake a hot biscuit with any left over. Bake in a 400° oven for 30–40 minutes. It will take longer if the fruit is cold and will not be as light. *Serves 6-8*

° My New England Grandmother's Apple Dumpling

This is really an apple cobbler and differs from a deep-dish apple pie only in the crust, which is drop biscuit dough and not pastry. Serve it with molasses or ice cream.

5-6 medium-size apples
½-⅔ cup sugar, depending on
    tartness of apples
¼ teaspoon cinnamon
⅛ teaspoon nutmeg

¼ cup raisins, preferably golden
    (optional)
2 tablespoons butter
½ recipe for shortcake (page 203)

Lightly grease a baking dish about 9 inches in diameter and 3 inches deep. Peel, core, and slice apples as for a pie. Fill the baking dish to within 1 inch of rim. Mix sugar, cinnamon, nutmeg, and raisins into apple slices. Dot with butter. Make shortcake dough and drop it by spoonfuls onto the apples. Bake in a 400° oven for 20 minutes. Reduce heat to 350° F. and bake 30 minutes more.   *Serves 6.*

° Green Tomato Pie

4-5 really green tomatoes
Pastry for 8-inch 2-crust pie
1½ cups brown sugar
3 tablespoons flour
Grated rind of 1 lemon

6 tablespoons lemon juice
½ cup golden raisins
¼ teaspoon salt
¼ teaspoon allspice
¼ cup minced candied ginger

Put tomatoes through a coarse grater. I use the large shredder of my food processor. There should be 2½ cups. Put in a colander and let drain overnight. Or prepare tomatoes in the morning and press the juices out of them from time to time through the day.

Prepare your favorite double pie crust, roll out half and put in an 8-inch pie pan. Roll out the other half and set aside. Mix remaining ingredients with tomatoes, place in pie shell, and cover with top crust. Prick holes in it. Bake in a 450° oven for 10 minutes, then reduce heat to 350° and cook 40 minutes longer.   *Makes one 8″ pie.*

○*Carrot Drop Cookies*

1 egg, beaten
⅓ cup cooking oil
⅓ cup sugar
¾ cup all-purpose flour
**⅔ teaspoon double-acting baking
  powder**
¼ teaspoon salt

1 teaspoon grated orange rind
**½ cup finely grated carrot, cooked
  2 minutes in boiling water and
  drained**
⅓ cup golden raisins
¼ teaspoon cumin

Preheat the oven to 350° F. Beat the egg, oil, and sugar together. Add the remaining ingredients and mix well. Drop from a teaspoon onto a greased cookie sheet. Space generously. Bake 10–12 minutes, or until cookies are golden brown. *Makes about 30 cookies*

10

The
Whole
Meal.

PARKER LEIGHTON

Experience, which is a patient teacher, has taught me to plan a meal and look at the plan from the angles of compatibility of flavors and textures, preparation time, stove space, serving dishes, appearance on plates, and ease of serving.

Plan on serving dishes that require different cooking times, especially when they need a lot of stirring at the start. When entertaining, avoid recipes that call for much last-minute attention or additions. If this cannot be avoided, at least have the ingredients measured and handy to use.

I prefer to serve roasts or braised meats or casseroles which can be prepared ahead of time and, except for occasional basting, require little from me toward mealtime.

The vegetables do have to wait for last-minute cooking, but they should be ready for the pot. A kettle of hot water waits for them on the stove. If I choose to serve more than one vegetable, I select a root crop, such as beets or carrots, and a green vegetable.

Most of my meals start with a salad or melon, and the ingredients for the salad are washed and dried ahead of time, wrapped in a clean dish towel, and placed in the refrigerator waiting to be put in the salad bowl at the last minute. Tomatoes or other wet vegetables, of course, are in a bowl. I usually serve cottage cheese with salads. Sweet fruit molds do not appeal to me except as desserts.

When the main course of a meal is heavy, i.e., with pork, ham, or beef, I usually choose a refreshing dessert light in calories. Should I serve my family a meal using leftovers, which I think are some of the tastiest meals, I prepare a nice, pretty dessert such as a fruit cobbler or tart.

Before I present some menus, I'll give you a few ideas for starting the meal—dips and soups—and a couple of casseroles that make simple meals utilizing leftovers.

Dips

You can really have fun making dips, because it is pronounced flavor you are after. I try to bring out the taste of a specific herb or vegetable, and I serve the dips with raw vegetables in place of chips or crackers.

A platter of fresh or crisp-cooked vegetables has rapidly become a staple of cocktail parties in this country. When you gather the vegetables from your garden, arrange them attractively, and serve them with one or more of the following dips, you are sure to please everyone.

Choose from these vegetables: carrot and celery sticks; cucumber "fingers"; strips of green pepper; scallions; cherry tomatoes; radishes; slices of turnip, celeriac, and kohlrabi; snap peas; cauliflower and broccoli flowerets; button mushrooms; watercress; zucchini; raw or crisp-cooked tiny green beans.

ᵒ *Artichoke Relish Dip*

Jerusalem Artichoke Relish (see recipe, page 192) mixed with an equal amount of cream cheese is very good with slices of kohlrabi.

°Golden Beet Dip

About 3 medium-size golden beets
Salt
6 leaves fresh basil, chopped
2 rounded tablespoons chopped
  fresh dill

2 tablespoons white vinegar
2 cups sour cream

Cook beets until just tender, then peel and grate on a medium grater. You should have about 2 cups. Sprinkle salt on beets. Mix the basil, dill, vinegar, and sour cream in a blender. Fold grated beets into the sour cream mix. When serving, sprinkle a little more dill on top.   *Makes about 4 cups*

°Curried Vegetable Dip

Make this about half an hour before serving. It is good with carrots, raw cauliflower, sliced kohlrabi, or turnips.

1 cup mayonnaise
2 teaspoons tarragon vinegar
Dash of pepper
½ teaspoon salt
⅛ teaspoon thyme

½ teaspoon curry powder
2 teaspoons chili sauce
2 teaspoons chopped chives or
  fennel
2 tablespoons grated onion

Combine all ingredients and mix well.   *Makes about 1 cup*

°A Dip with a Touch of the Near East

The mixture of sorrel and savory was called *zatre* when I lived in Palestine. Serve this with fingers of zucchini, slices of kohlrabi, or strips of sweet peppers.

1½ cups ricotta cheese
1 tablespoon finely chopped sorrel

2 teaspoons chopped winter savory
  or 3 teaspoons summer savory
1 tablespoon olive oil

Mix all together.   *Makes about 1½ cups*

°Eggplant Dip

Serve with sections of different-colored sweet peppers or pieces of flat Arabic bread for scoops.

1 large eggplant
2 medium-size tomatoes, peeled
⅛-¼ cup olive oil
1 clove garlic, crushed
1 onion, peeled and chopped
1 large green or red pepper,
   chopped

2 tablespoons dry red wine or 1
   tablespoon lemon juice
1 teaspoon cumin seed or 1
   tablespoon finely chopped basil
1 teaspoon fresh hot red pepper or
   ⅛ teaspoon black pepper
1 teaspoon salt

Bake eggplant whole in a 400° oven for 1 hour, or until soft. Let it cool and scoop out the flesh. Combine the eggplant with the tomatoes and chop in the food processor (don't purée—leave it chunky) or by hand.

Heat olive oil in a fry pan. Sauté garlic, onion, and pepper for a few minutes. Remove garlic and mix the rest with the eggplant mixture. Add remaining ingredients, mix thoroughly, and let sit overnight. *Makes 3 cups.*

°Quick Summer Squash Dip

Serve this with carrot sticks or sliced raw vegetables. The Krazy Salt seasoning, a mixture of salt, pepper, herbs, and lemon rind, is very handy to have on the seasoning rack.

8-ounce package cream cheese,
   softened
1 cup yogurt
1 cup coarsely grated raw yellow
   summer squash

1 tablespoon lemon juice
1 teaspoon Jane's Krazy Mixed up
   Salt, or more to taste

Combine all the ingredients. *Makes about 2½ cups*

Soups

The first fun I had in cooking was in making soups—it was a challenge to see what I could concoct with leftovers in the refrigerator.

There are two classes of soups: those that are good as an introduction to a meal and those that are really the main part of a meal, as for lunch with a simple sandwich.

For introductory soups I like light ones that have a simple flavor, such as the following. The ones made with tomato juice are good before a meal of red meat or fresh pork. The ones with chicken broth are good starters for a fish or poultry dinner.

°Hot Tomato Juice

To dress this up, you can mix some parsley or chives with softened cream cheese and float a spoonful of it on top. To thicken a bit, add a teaspoon of minute tapioca to the cold juice before heating.

2 cups tomato juice	**¼ teaspoon dried basil, or 2-3**
1 teaspoon sugar	**fresh basil leaves**
1 tablespoon finely chopped celery	**½ teaspoon butter**

Mix all the ingredients and heat. Remove basil leaves before serving.

Serves 2

○ *Carrot and Tomato Broth*

You may add other flavors to the broth if you wish, such as a different herb, a shake of herb-seasoned salt, or a pinch of coriander. I like to use this to start a meal which includes red meat or fresh pork.

1½ cups tomato juice
1 cup carrot juice
2 teaspoons chopped parsley

1 teaspoon butter
½ teaspoon chicken bouillon
   crystals (optional)

Combine all ingredients, adding bouillon crystals if tomato and carrot juice have not been salted. *Serves 2-3*

○ *Chicken Broth and Puréed Green Peas*

This is a good time to use, as I do, a cube of frozen chicken broth flavored with tarragon.

1¾ cups chicken broth
1 cup puréed cooked fresh or
   canned green peas
½ cup cream or undiluted
   evaporated milk

Salt, if needed
2 tablespoons dry white wine
1 tablespoon finely chopped green
   lettuce (optional)

Combine broth, peas, cream or milk, and salt and just heat through—do not boil. Before serving, stir in the wine. For color you may add lettuce. *Serves 3-4*

○ *Chicken Broth and Zucchini*

Any leftover zucchini or zucchini casserole put through the blender and added to chicken broth seasoned with a cube of frozen broth with tarragon makes a good light soup. Of course, this can be made with fresh zucchini also. Garnish with chives.

◦ *Mixed Vegetable Soup*

If I have a variety of leftover vegetables or small quantities of fresh vegetables, I make a vegetable soup using any meat stock I have. Stock may be made with bouillon cubes, using 1 cube to 2 cups water.

For two servings use 1¼ cups chopped vegetables for 2 cups stock. If the stock was made with beef bones, I like to add some tomato to it.

I think a good, hearty soup should have rice or cooked dried beans or a pasta in it. My choice is fine noodles broken up. Cook these in the stock first before adding cooked vegetables. If you wish to use cooked meat in the soup, add it just before serving. When you use ground beef, brown it first in a pan, pour the fat off, then add the meat to the soup.

The vegetables should be a pleasing combination of yellow and green. For yellow, use carrots, golden beets, yellow turnips, or yellow squash. For green, use string beans, lima beans, zucchini, green celery and leaves, shredded greens of any kind, and parsley or chives. Oregano and savory or mixed salad herbs may be used. If you don't have some sweet red peppers to add, use paprika. If the soup just doesn't pull together, add 2 tablespoons butter and 1 teaspoon sugar.

A rich vegetable soup is good served with a broiled-fish dinner, or as the main course for lunch with French bread and butter or a sandwich.

° *Minestrone*

This soup is not made with a meat stock, so the preparation of the browned vegetables is most important—they give the soup liquor its flavor.

1 stalk celery, strings removed,
   with lots of leaves
1 onion, 2 inches in diameter
1 very small clove garlic
1 slice cooked bacon

3 large basil leaves
1½ tablespoons oil
¾ cup canned or soaked small
   dried beans (I prefer canned)

Chop the celery, onion, garlic, bacon, and basil together until they are a mushy mass. In a 3- or 4-quart pot with a heavy bottom, heat the oil and add the chopped mixture. Stir it around now and then. The vegetables must be browned but not scorched. Add 5 cups water and the beans. If using dried beans, cook for 30 minutes before adding the following vegetables, all cut up in pieces that are no larger than the width of a teaspoon. Use a food processor, if you have one, to save time.

1 good-size carrot
1 celery stalk
1 medium potato, raw or cooked
1 medium onion
½-¾ cup chopped skinned tomato
Half an 8-inch zucchini

1 cup green beans
¼ cup broken-up macaroni
¼ cup green peas (if you have
   them)
1 teaspoon celery salt or plain salt

Cook for 45 minutes. Ten minutes before serving, add:

1 cup flavorful green leafy
   vegetable: green cabbage, chard,
   mustard greens, escarole, or
   spinach cut in short, thin strips

When serving, top with:

¾ cup thinly sliced peperoni or
   Polish sausage, cooked crisp

Sprinkling of Parmesan cheese

Serves 6

°Vegetable Cream Soups

To make cream soups, use half chicken stock and half milk as well as ⅓ cup powdered milk for each cup of stock.

If you are not going to use precooked vegetables, cook fresh vegetables in the stock. Cut the vegetables in equal-size pieces and, when using greens, be sure they are in short, narrow pieces, not long strings.

For a good white color, when thickening use 1¼ tablespoons flour for each cup of liquid. Mix the flour and powdered milk together and stir some cold stock in slowly. Add hot stock to it and stir well over medium heat until the flour is cooked, being sure there are no lumps. Add the milk and heat, but do not boil or cover. Add the cooked vegetables, heat through, then season and serve.

I season my cream soup with chicken bouillon crystals or celery salt, 1 scant teaspoon for 2 cups liquid.

Suggested additions to 2 cups cream-soup base might be 1 cup diced carrot and celery and 2 teaspoons chopped parsley; or 1 cup chopped cooked cauliflower, a pinch of ginger, some sweet pepper or paprika for color, and a sprinkle of seasoned bread crumbs on top. Use your imagination, or try the following chowder.

°Vegetable Fish Chowder

I like to make a fish chowder with leftover fish and vegetables, but of course it can be made from scratch.

3 cups cream soup (see above)
½ cup diced cooked potatoes
¼ cup chopped onion
¼ cup chopped celery leaves
¼ cup shredded carrot
1 tablespoon sweet red pepper (optional)

¾ cup or more seasoned cooked fish
1 teaspoon butter (optional)
Paprika

Heat soup base, potatoes, onion, celery leaves, carrot, and pepper (if you wish to use it) in the top of a double boiler. Break fish in bits and add it to the soup just before serving. Heat through, but do not

boil. If fish had no butter on it already, add the butter. Shake paprika on top. *Serves 3-4*

∘*Cream of Corn Soup*

1 cup scraped or creamed corn	Salt to taste
2 cups milk	Scant teaspoon sugar (optional)
1 teaspoon butter	Dash of white pepper (optional)
1 tablespoon finely chopped onion	
1 teaspoon chopped parsley or chives (optional)	

Put ½ cup of the corn in blender with 1 cup milk and blend until
smooth. Mix all the corn, milk, and butter together in the top of a
double boiler over boiling water and let it simmer for at least 30
minutes. It will get thicker the longer it simmers. A few minutes
before serving, add onion, herb, and salt. If you are using old corn,
you may want to add the sugar, and you might like a dash of pepper.

Serves 3.

∘*Purée of Squash Soup*

When serving this as a cold soup, use chopped sorrel in place of the
cumin seed, or serve with a lemon wedge.

1 tablespoon butter	¼ teaspoon cumin seed, mixed salad herbs, chopped sorrel, or lemon wedges
3 cups diced summer squash	
½ cup chopped onion	
1¼ cups milk	½ tablespoon chives
½ teaspoon (or more) chicken-broth crystals	Paprika or chopped fresh sweet red pepper

Sauté squash and onion until raw taste has gone. Put in blender or
food processor with remaining ingredients and blend until puréed.
Heat and serve, or serve cold. *Serves 3-4.*

○ *Purée of Carrot Soup*

Two 7-inch carrots about 1 inch in diameter, sliced	½ teaspoon salt
	3 pinches of ground coriander
⅛ teaspoon dried tarragon or 2 sprigs fresh, or a cube of tarragon-flavored frozen chicken stock	2 cups chicken stock
	⅓ cup evaporated milk
	Chopped parsley

Cook carrots, tarragon, salt, and coriander in stock until carrots are tender. Remove tarragon sprigs. Purée in blender or food processor until smooth. Put in a pot and add the milk. Heat and garnish with chopped parsley before serving.   *Serves 3.*

Casseroles

I enjoy putting together a casserole dish almost as much as making a soup. Soup I can taste as I add ingredients, but with casseroles I have to mentally taste the flavors and textures. Creating a picture with the ingredients as I place them in the dish is fun. If it looks dull I add a spot of color with parsley, fresh red pepper, or a slice of tomato. Even shredded carrot is effective. I place broccoli or asparagus at one end to feature it.

Often the success of a casserole depends as much on what is not used as on what is. Do not always add cheese for a topping. Sometimes use crushed dry stuffing cubes or herb-seasoned crumbs and dot with butter. When serving a casserole containing fish add a little dry white wine a few minutes before serving.

○ *Chicken and Vegetable Casserole*

One day by chance I had all the following ingredients, except the rice, in my refrigerator and made a casserole with them. It was so good that I made it later from scratch, not from leftovers, for a garden-club luncheon. I use a cube of my rosemary-flavored stock in this; you could also season the stock with celery. Serve with Frozen Cranberry Relish (see recipe) and a green salad.

⅔ cup rice, cooked in well-
  seasoned chicken stock
2 fresh pimentos, chopped, or 1
  sweet red pepper, chopped
½ cup chopped cooked carrots
½ cup chopped cooked celery
½ cup creamed corn

¾ can cream of mushroom soup
¼ cup snipped parsley
4 cups cubed cooked chicken
1 cup milk
¼ cup stuffing mix or dry bread
  crumbs
1 tablespoon butter (optional)

Mix all together except stuffing or crumbs, adding butter if the vegetables don't already have butter on them. Put in a casserole and top
with stuffing or crumbs. Bake in a 350° oven for 45 minutes or until
heated through.　　　　　　　　　　　　　　　　　　　　　　　*Serves 5.*

∘ *Creamed Vegetable Casserole*

Any number of vegetables can be mixed in this hearty hot lunch
dish, but I prefer to use broccoli or spinach separately. When using
broccoli, ¼ teaspoon cumin seed (instead of coriander or curry) adds
an interesting flavor.

2 cups cooked vegetables
1 hard-boiled egg cut in small
  wedges
2 cups Basic White Sauce (page 30)
1 tablespoon snipped parsley
  (except with spinach)

1 tablespoon snipped chives
¼ teaspoon ground coriander or
  curry powder (optional)
1 cup biscuit mix
Grated Parmesan cheese

Mix vegetables, egg, white sauce, parsley, chives, and coriander or
curry. Heat in a deep casserole, then make drop biscuit dough, using biscuit mix, and drop it in small dabs over the hot vegetables.
Sprinkle Parmesan cheese on top and bake in a 375° oven until
biscuit is baked.　　　　　　　　　　　　　　　　　　　　　*Serves 4-5.*

Menus

The following menus will give you some idea of my choice of combinations. The main entrées are ones I have frequently served to
guests or are family favorites.

AN ELEGANT FISH DINNER

- Mixed green salad of romaine and another type of lettuce, celery heart including leaves, and diced Golden Beet Pickle (page 78)
- Fordhook Fish
- Tenderpod or Romano green beans
- Cooked diced carrots and celery with butter and parsley
- Blueberry Crumb Pudding (page 206)

◦ Fordhook Fish

This dish, a variation of sole véronique, was Mr. Burpee's favorite fish dish.

1 pound fresh or frozen fillets of sole, flounder, or fluke	¼ teaspoon salt
5 tablespoons butter or margarine	Freshly ground pepper (optional)
⅓ cup golden raisins, packed lightly, or 1 cup peeled seedless grapes	½ teaspoon chopped parsley
	3 tablespoons flour
	1½ cups freshly mashed potatoes
1 small onion, sliced wafer thin	About ¾ cup milk or light cream
½ cup semidry white wine	2 tablespoons grated Parmesan cheese

Rinse fish fillets and pat dry; thaw frozen fillets and pat dry. Place a large piece of heavy foil on a shallow pan. Dot center with 1 tablespoon butter or margarine. Place fillets on foil and arrange raisins or grapes and onion slices over fish. Pour the wine over top. Dot fish with a second tablespoon of butter and sprinkle with salt, pepper, and parsley. Seal the foil over the fish and bake at 400° F. for 20 minutes, no more.

While fish bakes, melt the remaining butter in a small saucepan, blend in the flour, and cook gently 3–4 minutes. Have well-seasoned hot mashed potatoes ready. Remove fish from oven. Open one end of foil and gently pour juice little by little into butter-flour mixture. Add milk or cream to make 2 cups sauce. Stir and cook to not quite medium-thick consistency. Add additional seasonings to taste.

Transfer foil with fillets to a heatproof platter. Spread out foil to shape of dish and crimp to make attractive edging. Pour one-third of the sauce around the fish and try to get some under it. Spoon mashed potatoes around the fish and pour the remainder of the sauce over fish. Sprinkle with grated cheese and brown lightly under broiler.

Serves 3-4

A HEARTY SUPPER WITH CHICKEN OR LAMB STEW

Unfortunately, many people when they think of a stew recall a mouthful of gristly or fatty meat. This should not be so and need not be so when the meat is prepared properly. It takes time to prepare a good stew, but I enjoy thinking of the flavor and the fact that all the kitchen mess will have been cleaned up long before I sit down to the table. My family prefers chicken and lamb stew to beef, but if you make beef stew, it calls, I think, for some tomato, a bay leaf, and turnip or rutabaga.

- Mixed lettuce salad with young celery leaves, onion rings, and cubes of tomato aspic
- Chicken stew with celery, carrots, beans or peas, whole small onions, red peppers, and summer savory
- Hot cornbread or candied buttercup squash
- Chopped boiled chard with butter

OR

- Lamb stew with same vegetables as chicken stew, but rosemary instead of savory
- Potatoes boiled in jackets, peeled and cubed while hot, and broiled with butter and parsley for a few minutes
- Sautéed Zucchini with Herbs (see page 119)

- Dessert for either meal: Mixed fruit, fresh or frozen, such as a combination of peaches and strawberries or raspberries and blueberries
- Cookies or pound cake

∘ *Chicken or Lamb Stew*

Buy a whole chicken or a whole shoulder of lamb. Cook it in water seasoned with two sprigs fresh rosemary or four sprigs summer savory and a little salt. Let the pot simmer, not boil for 45–60 minutes. You can tell when chicken is done by moving the legs—they should move freely. Lamb is done when it is fork-tender. It is better to undercook than overcook stew meat, for if overcooked it is tasteless and becomes stringy when reheated just before serving. If it seems to be undercooked when you separate it into smaller pieces, don't worry—it will get further cooking. Cook the meat the day before you plan to serve the stew. Let the meat cool in its broth overnight.

The next day discard the herbs and skim off the fat. With your fingers separate the meat from the bones, fat, and gristle, using a knife as little as possible. Refrigerate. (It sounds like a lot of work, but the result is worth it.)

Prepare the vegetables: Cut the carrots and celery into 3-inch pieces; spear the small onions with a toothpick across the rings so they will stay whole; peel and cut up the pieces of red or green pepper. If you don't have celery, add celery flakes and use stalks of chard. Cook the vegetables in the stew broth. Add peas or green beans shortly before serving. Thicken the broth with flour, add the meat, and heat on medium temperature. Add fresh chopped parsley, taste for seasoning, and serve.

A ROAST LAMB DINNER

- Mixed lettuce salad with fresh tomatoes (or tomato aspic) and cottage cheese
- Roast lamb
- Carrots and onions braised with lamb
- Lyonnaise or mashed potatoes
- Frozen fruits

° Roast Lamb

Remove all but a thin layer of fat from the lamb roast as well as the grayish glands which are hidden in the fat underneath the wider end. Insert slivers of garlic (2 cloves are plenty) into the flesh and rub meat with flour and celery salt. Fresh mint or rosemary placed on top of the roast while cooking gives a pleasant aroma to the kitchen and the meat. Crushed dried rosemary may be rubbed onto the roast before putting it in the oven.

Put lamb in a roaster with a cover. First sear under broiler, then add ½ cup water to pan, cover, and roast at 350° F. for 25 minutes per pound of meat. (I like lamb well done). An hour before serving, add carrots cut in half lengthwise, onions pierced across with toothpicks (remove when serving), and a little water if there is no liquid in pan for basting vegetables, which should be done twice. Remove roast from oven and uncover it 15 minutes before serving for flesh to firm up for better carving. If you want to make gravy, put roast and vegetables on a heated platter and cover with foil.

° Frozen Fruits

When serving mixed frozen fruits, remember that peaches take longer to thaw than berries; strawberries take longer than blueberries or raspberries, which take almost no time at all. Thaw in your refrigerator in a bowl so the thawing will be more even.

A VEGETARIAN MEAL

○ Mixed cold marinated string beans, golden beets, and carrots, with some diced celery and onion, served on a bed of lettuce

OR

○ Marinated diced red beets, chopped celery and onion, fresh dill, and chopped hard-boiled egg on lettuce
○ Eggplant and Rice Casserole
○ Boiled golden beet tops seasoned with cream of mushroom soup
○ Fordhook Pudding or Trifle

○ Eggplant and Rice Casserole

8 slices young eggplant, ½ inch thick	6 slices peeled tomato
½ cup chopped onion	4 fresh basil leaves
Vegetable oil	Salt
½ cup rice	Butter
1¼ cups chicken broth	Cracker or fine dry bread crumbs
	Grated Parmesan cheese

Lightly brown eggplant and onion in a little oil. Cook rice in chicken broth. Place half the eggplant slices and onion in the bottom of a greased 1½-quart casserole. Place 3 tomato slices and 2 basil leaves on top. Sprinkle with salt. Now spread half the rice on top and repeat the layers. Top with dabs of butter, crumbs, and a sprinkling of Parmesan cheese. Bake in preheated 350° oven for 30 minutes.

Serves 4.

○ Fordhook Pudding or Trifle

Prepare this ahead of time. Put cubes of a berry gelatin and cubes of layer cake or any leftover white cake in individual glass dessert dishes. Pour a soft custard on top while it is warm so that it will soak into the cake but not melt the gelatin. Top with fresh or frozen berries just before serving.

A LUNCH OR LIGHT SUPPER OF CHICKEN GIBLETS

- Bowl of green salad with marinated vegetables
- Rozz Dumyat (chicken giblet rice, an African dish)
- Cheesecake with Rhubarb-Pineapple Sauce (page 202)

∘ *Rozz Dumyat*

Have you looked at the price of a package of chicken giblets recently? Once I acquired a lot of giblets when I prepared a chicken dish for a number of people. I thought I should be able to use them other than in gravy, so I went on a hunt for a giblet recipe. I found only one in my many cookbooks and have made an adaptation of it. It's a great dish for preparing ahead of time and serving for a simple supper, after a late-afternoon meeting, with a tossed salad. So save the giblets when you serve fried or broiled chicken; put them in a container and freeze for use in Rozz Dumyat.

1 pound chicken or turkey giblets, preferably only a few livers	1 cup rice
	1 cup finely diced celery
Sprig of savory	3 cups chicken broth or bouillon
1 tablespoon pine nuts	1 teaspoon salt if unsalted broth
2 tablespoons butter	used
⅓ cup seedless raisins	⅛ cup dry white wine (optional)

Cook giblets in water with a sprig of winter savory. If you don't have winter savory, use summer savory. Remove sprig after cooking. Save cooking liquid for the rice. Drain giblets, remove gristle from gizzards, and chop. Brown nuts slightly in 1 tablespoon butter.

Wash and drain raisins. Combine raisins in 3-quart saucepan with nuts and giblets. Add rice, celery, remaining butter, chicken broth or bouillon, and salt if necessary. Cover and cook over moderate heat for 45 minutes. The mixture should be fluffy and nearly dry. Test for seasoning. Just before serving, you may pour the wine over the dish for an overtone flavor. ***Serves 4.***

AN ARABIC LUNCHEON

Served with a bowl of green salad, kibbee is a complete meal that is easy to serve to a crowd.

○ *Kibbee*

Kibbee, my favorite of the Arabic main-meal dishes, was served only on special occasions when I lived in Palestine, perhaps because it took so long to make. The Arab women did not have meat grinders, so they sat on the floor and with wooden pestles pounded the meat into mincemeat, then pounded the wheat into it. They used lamb or goat meat, as beef was very, very scarce. I use a mixture of beef and lamb. Instead of bulgur you could use a packaged pilaf and its seasonings (if it has them) instead of cinnamon and allspice.

½ pound bulgur
1½ cups water
1 pound ground beef
1 pound ground lamb
2 teaspoons salt
1 teaspoon cinnamon

1 teaspoon allspice
4 medium-large onions, chopped
  and sautéed in fat
1 cup pine nuts, lightly toasted, or
  chopped cashews
1 envelope dehydrated onion soup

Put the bulgur and water in a heavy pot, bring to a boil, and simmer 10 minutes or until the water is absorbed. The bulgur should still be firm. Mix it with the beef, lamb, salt, cinnamon, and allspice, then divide the mixture in half. Spread half the meat mixture in the bottom of a baking pan about 9x11 inches and at least 1½ inches deep. Press it down firmly. It should be ½ inch thick.

    Mix onions and nuts together and spread over the meat layer in the pan. Make a top layer with the remaining half of the meat mixture and press firmly. Shake dehydrated onion soup over the top. Bake for 45 minutes in a 400° oven. Cut in squares or diamonds and serve hot.   *Serves 10.*

AN UNUSUAL CHICKEN SALAD FOR LUNCH

- ° Oven Chicken Salad
- ° Rolls
- ° Molded fruit salad of your choice

°*Oven Chicken Salad*

2 cups diced cooked chicken, preferably white meat
¾ cup diced celery, strings removed
¼ cup chopped red and/or green peppers
8-ounce can water chestnuts, drained and sliced
3½-ounce can French-fried onions
2 tablespoons mayonnaise

1 teaspoon dry Good Seasons Old-Fashioned French Salad Dressing
1½ tablespoons chopped chives
1½ tablespoons chopped parsley
1½ cups Basic White Sauce (page 30) made with milk and seasoned with chicken-broth crystals, a pinch of thyme, white pepper, and paprika

Mix all ingredients (except half the onions) together in a large bowl. Pour into oiled 1-quart baking dish. Sprinkle rest of onions over top and bake in preheated 400° oven 15 minutes or until hot through.   *Serves 4-5*

A MAKE-AHEAD DINNER

When your guests are traveling and you do not know at what time dinner will be served, I recommend preparing Chicken Cacciatore because it can be set aside and warmed up. The rice could be brown rice cooked and held in a steamer over hot water, since brown rice does not get gummy. Have in the refrigerator the makings for a green salad ready to put together.

- ○ Mixed green salad
- ○ Chicken Cacciatore
- ○ Rice or Kasha
- ○ Fruit pie

○Chicken Cacciatore

2 pounds chicken legs, drumsticks and thighs separated
2 tablespoons shortening
10¾-ounce can tomato soup
¾ cup chopped onion
2 large cloves garlic, minced (if you don't like garlic, use more onion)
1 teaspoon crushed fresh oregano or ½ teaspoon dry
¼ teaspoon salt
2 green or red peppers, peeled and cut in pieces 1¼ inch wide
¼ cup dry sherry or red wine

Brown the chicken in shortening in a heavy fry pan. Pour off fat. Add the other ingredients except peppers and wine. Cook over low heat for 30 minutes covered. Stir now and then. Add wine and peppers. Mix them in and cook 15 minutes more.   *Serves 4*

At the Table

Eye appeal has a great deal to do with taste appeal and the enjoyment of a meal. After I have chosen my menu I decide which of my dishes I will use and then which placemats. When the meal is colorful I use plain off-white china on neutral-colored placemats, such as tones of pale green and light blue. When serving fish or roasts, I use more decorative china on natural-colored placemats.

I decide on flowers next, and take the time to prepare an arrangement the day before if I'm giving a party. When people are seated, the arrangement should be low enough for them to see over it when looking across the table. When flowers are scarce, vegetables, fruits, and leaves substitute as table decorations. I have used only herbs—they can look lovely with their varying shades of green and gray, and you can invite your guests to eat them too.

Seating of guests is often overlooked today, but it is also a secret of an enjoyable meal. Do let your guests have the better view when eating outdoors. Mix couples up and do not let one guest dominate the conversation. My husband was very clever in breaking in diplomatically with an amusing story which he had up his sleeve ready to pull out at an appropriate time. When he thought there had been enough serious horticultural talk, one of his favorites was: "Do you know what was the first hybrid known to man? It was the mule, and you know what a useful animal it is. It amazes me how slow plant breeders were to realize the value of hybrids. That cross between the jackass and the mare was made thousands of years ago, and I believe it was the jackass's own idea." The way he said it always brought laughter.

Another favorite was an old Chinese proverb:

"If you want to be happy for an hour—get drunk.
If you want to be happy for a day—get married.
If you want to be happy for a week—kill your pig and eat it.
If you want to be happy all life long—become a gardener . . ."

Then with a twinkle in his eye and a spontaneous chorus from the guests he would add, "and plant Burpee seeds."

Index

Entries in italics refer to gardening information.

Entries in italics refer to gardening information.

Entries in italics refer to gardening information.

Entries in italics refer to gardening information.

Entries in italics refer to gardening information.

Entries in italics refer to gardening information.

Entries in italics refer to gardening information.

Entries in italics refer to gardening information.

Entries in italics refer to gardening information.

Entries in italics refer to gardening information.

Entries in italics refer to gardening information.

Entries in italics refer to gardening information.

Entries in italics refer to gardening information.